LIVING STONES

ROCKS

SUSAN SAYERS

Illustrated by
Arthur Baker

Kevin Mayhew

First published in 1997
This revised edition published in 2000 by
KEVIN MAYHEW LTD
Buxhall
Stowmarket
Suffolk IP14 3BW

5 6 7 8 9

ISBN 1 84003 011 9
Catalogue No. 1500115

The other titles in the *Living Stones* series are

Complete Resource Book	ISBN 1 84003 009 7	Cat. No. 1500113
Prayers of Intercession	ISBN 1 84003 013 5	Cat. No. 1500117
Pebbles	ISBN 1 84003 010 0	Cat. No. 1500114
Boulders	ISBN 1 84003 012 7	Cat. No. 1500116

Cover photographs:
Group of children – courtesy of SuperStock Ltd, London
Background – courtesy of Images Colour Library Ltd, London
Cover design by Jaquetta Sergeant
Edited by Katherine Laidler
Typesetting by Louise Selfe
Printed in Great Britain

Foreword

For children of primary school age the sense of belonging to a peer group becomes increasingly important. Their faith development can be fostered in group activities which are fun and challenging. Their growing awareness of the wider world is often linked with a strong sense of justice and social responsibility, and they need to see the Christian perspective in all this.

Rocks encourages the children to begin thinking about the implications of their faith. Their participation in the story-telling and teaching is welcomed.

It would be wiser to split the group into two age groups, adapting the suggestions on the worksheets accordingly.

This is something of a DIY kit, supplied with plenty of openings to meet your own parish needs and the needs of the children, and to spark off your own imaginative ideas. It is based on the belief that children are as much a part of the Church as adults, and that there is great value in sharing the same teaching each Sunday whatever our age. This book follows the weekly readings of the Common Worship Lectionary (Principal Service) for Year C of the three-year cycle, so that the whole church will have that common experience.

Rocks includes a series of weekly activity sheets. These may be copied without further permission or charge for non-commercial use. They can be used as they stand, or you can select the material you want. Copy them for the children to take home, use them in church, put them in the magazine or news sheet, distribute them at clubs or Bible study groups, or use them in conjunction with your learning programme. They are 'working sheets' rather than 'work sheets' as they often include instructions for making and doing rather than being complete in themselves. Children will need their leaders to have planned ahead for the resources needed.

When planning for children's work it is advisable to read through the Bible passages prayerfully. You are then in a better position to see how the programme relates to the readings, and also to enable you to supplement and vary the programme as a result of your own insights and the specific needs of your group.

The children are encouraged to pray during the week, using the suggestions on their sheet. These can be built into a collection of prayers and made into a personal prayer book.

A few general ideas about story-telling:

- Tell the story from the viewpoint of a character in the situation. To create the time-machine effect, avoid eye contact as you slowly put on the appropriate cloth or cloak, and then make eye contact as you greet the children in character.
- Have an object with you which leads into the story – a water jug, or a lunch box, for instance.
- Walk the whole group through the story, so that they are physically moving from one place to another; and use all kinds of places, such as broom cupboards, under the stairs, outside under the trees, and so on.

- Collect some carpet tiles – blue and green – so that at story time the children can sit round the edge of this and help you place on the cut-outs for the story.

You may find it useful to keep a record of what you actually do each week, as well as build up a store of the resources you use, because this will obviously help to make future activities easier to prepare.

It is my hope that this book will not only stimulate ideas and enable a varied programme of children's work to take place, but most of all it will encourage us all, whatever our age, as we make the journey of faith together.

SUSAN SAYERS

ACKNOWLEDGEMENTS

The publishers wish to express their gratitude to Kingsway's Thankyou Music, PO Box 75, Eastbourne, East Sussex BN23 6NW, for permission to use the text and music of *Waiting for your Spirit*.

CONTENTS

Recommended Bibles

It is often a good idea to look at a passage in several different versions before deciding which to use for a particular occasion.

As far as children are concerned, separate Bible stories, such as those published by Palm Tree Press and Lion, are a good introduction for the very young. Once children are reading, a very helpful version is the *International Children's Bible* (New Century version) published by Word Publishing. Here children have a translation based on experienced scholarship, using language structure suitable for young readers, with short sentences and appropriate vocabulary. There is a helpful dictionary, and clear maps and pictures are provided.

ADVENT

First Sunday of Advent

Thought for the day

The gathered hopes of generations remind us to get ourselves ready, so that Christ's return will be a day of excitement and great joy.

Readings

Jeremiah 33:14-16
Psalm 25:1-10
1 Thessalonians 3:9-13
Luke 21:25-36

Aim

To help them understand that at Christmas we also look ahead to the second coming.

Starter

Split the group in two (or four if numbers are larger) and give the members of each group short strands of wool in their group's colour. All the children now drop or hide their wool all around the room. Now ask each group to find and collect a different colour. (First group back wins, if you want to add some competition.)

Teaching

Remind the children of how, when they were gathering up the wool, they were looking out for a particular type of wool, and only collecting that. We'll come back to this later.

They will all be aware that Christmas is approaching, and that we celebrate Jesus coming to live on earth as a human baby at that time. Enjoy the thought of Christmas coming.

Explain that while he was on earth, Jesus told us he would come back again one day and we will all be able to see him then. Make it quite clear that we have not been told when this will happen, and read Luke 21:25-28; 33-36, asking them to listen out for the signs to notice. Readers will find it helpful to follow the words using the worksheet.

Have a short 'Any questions?' slot at this point.

Now back to the wool gathering. At this second coming, all that is or has been good, honest, generous, kind, forgiving and loving will be gathered up or 'harvested', and last for ever. Jesus suggests that we make sure we are ready for this, so we can enjoy being part of the harvest.

Praying

Using the sprinter's 'Take your marks . . . get set . . . go!' actions, the children line up and crouch down,

Take me as I am, Lord Jesus,

raise themselves to the 'get set' position

make me more loving / forgiving / honest,

and run to the opposite wall

and use me for good!

Activities

Use the worksheet to work on ways to get ready and prepare for the time when all things will be fulfilled.

Notes

Jesus will come again in glory

Jesus said this:

'Amazing things will happen to the sun, moon and stars. On earth the nations will be afraid because of the roar and fury of the sea. They will not know what to do. People will be so afraid they will faint. They will wonder what is happening to the whole world. Everything in the sky will be changed.

Then people will see the Son of Man coming in a cloud with power and great glory.

When these things begin to happen don't fear. Look up and hold your heads high because the time when your God will free you is near!'

Do you think this is good news or bad news?

Underline the signs to notice in red.
Underline what people will see in blue.
Jesus says 'don't fear'.
Why don't we need to be afraid?
Underline the reason in green.

I want to be ready. I need God to help me with

To pray at home this week

Take me as I am,
Lord Jesus, make
me more loving
and use me
for good.
Amen.

Second Sunday of Advent

Thought for the day

It had been prophesied that there would be a messenger to prepare the way for the coming of the Messiah. Now John the Baptist appears with his urgent message of repentance.

Readings

Malachi 3:1-4
Canticle: Benedictus
Philippians 1:3-11
Luke 3:1-6

Aim

To understand that John was the prophesied forerunner to prepare the people for the Messiah.

Starter

Advance notice. Have a selection of posters and flyers for local events (the local press usually drops several on your floor as you open the paper each week). Have some with pictures to help non-readers. Have the posters at different places on the walls and give the children a minute to walk round and look at them. Then have everyone in the centre. Call out: 'Did you know there was going to be a circus next Saturday?' The children run to the appropriate poster.

Teaching

Beforehand prepare a poster that says: 'Good news – don't miss it! The Messiah is coming!' and a sign with a string attached saying 'John the Baptist'.

Explain that for thousands of years people had known that one day God would come among his people on earth in a very close way. The people of Israel were waiting for the day when the Messiah would appear on earth. (Display the poster.) Everyone can shout the message together. The name 'Messiah' means 'the chosen one' or 'the Christ'. But God didn't rely on posters: he went for a better idea. He went for a personal messenger.

At this point one of the leaders interrupts to say that she wants to give advance notice of a children's Christmas party / carol singing (or whatever exciting event you have planned for Christmas). The excitement generated by this will enable you to show how effective it is to have a personal messenger. Explain that the name of the personal messenger God chose was John, known as John the Baptist. (Hang the notice round the messenger's neck.)

What was John's message?

God told John to tell the people that to get ready for the coming Messiah, they needed to put their crooked lives straight. Their lives needed to be like clear firm roads. That meant sorting out all lying and cheating, all cruel and unkind behaviour, all mean and selfish living. The people wanted to get ready for the Messiah, so they wanted to sort their lives out. This turning away from sin is called 'repentance'. As a sign that their sins had been forgiven, John baptised the people in the water of the River Jordan. The people felt happy and free. It feels good to be forgiven.

Praying

Have everyone standing in a space facing the same direction. Whenever the leader says *Turn us round* the children turn around and continue with the prayer.

Father, whenever we are wanting our own way,
Turn us round to think of other people.

Whenever we know we are not being honest,
Turn us round to speak the truth.

Whenever we find ourselves being greedy,
Turn us round to share with others.

Thanks for helping, Lord.
Amen.

Activities

Use the worksheet to reinforce today's teaching and express the message of John in poster form for the rest of the congregation.

Notes

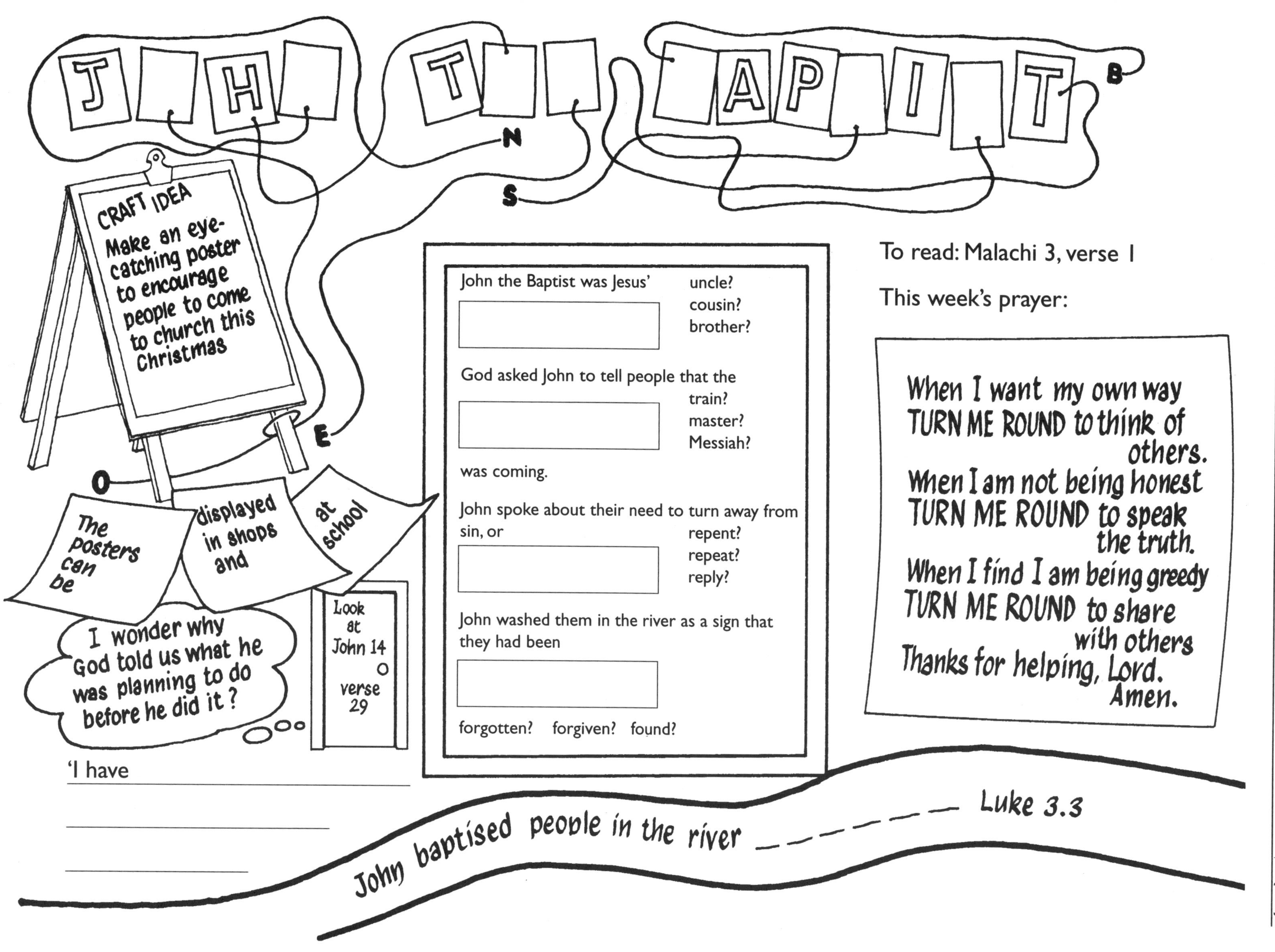

To read: Malachi 3, verse 1

This week's prayer:

When I want my own way
TURN ME ROUND to think of others.
When I am not being honest
TURN ME ROUND to speak the truth.
When I find I am being greedy
TURN ME ROUND to share with others
Thanks for helping, Lord.
Amen.

John the Baptist was Jesus' ______ uncle? cousin? brother?

God asked John to tell people that the ______ was coming. train? master? Messiah?

John spoke about their need to turn away from sin, or ______ repent? repeat? reply?

John washed them in the river as a sign that they had been ______ forgotten? forgiven? found?

THIRD SUNDAY OF ADVENT

Thought for the day

Our period of preparation shifts from repentance and forgiveness to the freed exhilaration of hope, as the momentous truth of God's immanence begins to dawn on us.

Readings

Zephaniah 3:14-20
Canticle: Isaiah 12:2-6
Philippians 4:4-7
Luke 3:7-18

Aim

To develop their understanding from last week about the importance of John as the forerunner to Christ.

Starter

Name and throw. Stand in a circle with a beach ball. Call out the name of someone else in the circle and then throw the ball to them. Remind them beforehand to see if they can make sure that everyone has at least one go. This activity helps build community, includes new children, and picks up on the fact that being chosen and called gets you ready to receive.

Teaching

Get the children to help recap the teaching from last week about who John was and why he was called the Baptist.

Have two leaders discussing what had gone on by the River Jordan when they were there in the crowd. One is a soldier and one a tax collector. To be able to do this effectively they will need to be very familiar with the Luke text and practise beforehand so that the conversation sounds natural and interesting while bringing out a) the teaching that John has given and b) their excitement about waiting for this other person John has told them to look out for.

Following the conversation, draw out the main points from the children, noting them on a flipchart, board or OHP.

Praying

Have this leader/response prayer shout, written up so everyone can join in:

Leader What do we want?

All We want to be ready!

Leader When do we want it?

All Now!

Leader Who can help us?

All God can help us

Leader When can he help us?

All Now!

Activities

Today's worksheet helps the children consolidate their understanding of the events at the River Jordan, placing them in their historical context. They can also make a stand-up model.

Notes

B	R	A	S	P	N	F	B
E	E	G	F	R	E	E	A
G	P	L	I	T	N	H	P
N	E	C	I	A	R	M	T
A	N	K	D	V	J	Q	I
H	T	R	I	V	E	R	S
C	O	O	L	D	S	E	T
J	O	H	N	U	A	P	E

JOHN the BAPTIST called people to REPENT and CHANGE what was wrong in their lives, so they could be SET FREE to LIVE. To show they were forgiven John baptised them in the RIVER JORDAN.

This week's prayer

Please Jesus help me to do whatever is right and good and honest today. Amen.

How to make the pop-up picture

1. Colour the picture
2. Cut out the people in the water, leaving the fold lines
3. Fold the back and people up like this

1. Find the River Jordan in an atlas.
2. What country is it in now?
3. Who was in charge when John was alive?

What did John say to the soldiers?

What did John say to the tax collectors?

Time Line

2000 Abraham lived — 0 Jesus lived — 2000 you live

Roman Empire

FOURTH SUNDAY OF ADVENT

Thought for the day

When we co-operate with God amazing things happen.

Readings

Micah 5:2-5a
Canticle: Magnificat or Psalm 80:1-7
Hebrews 10:5-10
Luke 1:39-45 (46-55)

Aim

To explore what it meant for Mary to say 'Yes'.

Starter

Either join with the younger children for parachute games, or have a team game which needs team members to co-operate (football is the obvious choice, or you could try French cricket or pass the balloon between the knees).

Teaching

Find out if anyone has ever been asked to play for the school team or orchestra, or sing in the choir. Have some pictures of well-known footballers and actors as well. Talk about how pleased and proud you feel to be asked to do an important job, but bring out the point that you can't just go along to play in the match or act in the performance. What other things would you have to do? List both the up- and the down-sides of such a privilege. Looking at it as a whole, would they still want to take it on? (You could vote on it.)

Have another sheet with a picture of Mary in the middle. It is headed, 'Chosen to be Jesus' mother'.

Look at what Mary was chosen for, and on one side of the picture list all the good things about it. Then think over Jesus' life and see if you can think of any sad, painful or difficult things that might be part of the job. List these on the other side of the picture. How would they feel about taking on the job?

At the bottom write, 'Mary still said "Yes!".' It amazed her that God had chosen her, and it made her realise how wonderful and sensible and patient and courageous God was to set about saving the world in this way.

Mary went to visit her cousin Elizabeth, who was six months pregnant with John the Baptist at the time, and both Mary and Elizabeth (and John) were filled with excitement and delight at what God was up to.

Praying

My soul glorifies the Lord
and my spirit rejoices in God my saviour.

Have some happy music on to dance to and while the music is still playing everyone claps a rhythm and shouts to it.

Activities

Consolidate the teaching using the worksheet and follow the instructions on it to make a Christmas table decoration.

Notes

God with us

A Christmas table decoration

You will need:
- a foil dish • a candle
- a chunk of oasis
- some holly and ivy
- some garden wire
- shiny coloured paper
- putty from a florist

How you make it

1 Cut out circles of shiny paper. Stick them back to back on short pieces of garden wire like this.

2 Fix the oasis in the foil dish with putty.

3 Push the candle and holly and ivy and garden wire berries into the oasis.

4 Decorate the 'God with us' label and stick it on the foil dish.

Mary knew it would not be an easy job being the mother of God's son.

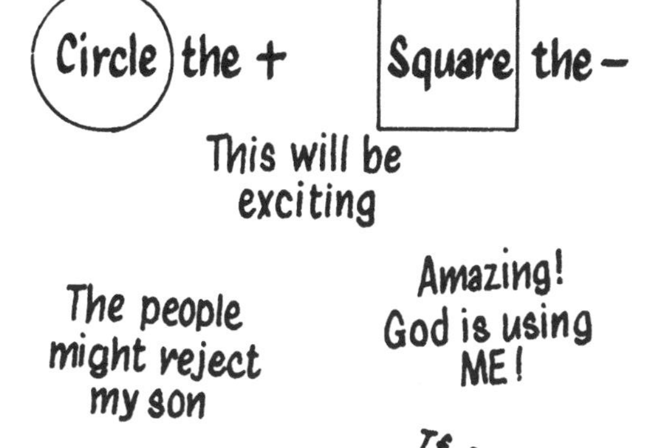

But... she still said:

Circle the + Square the –

This will be exciting

The people might reject my son

Amazing! God is using ME!

This is a mammoth job and I might do it wrong

If God has asked me I know he will help me to do it

People will not understand my son

God is keeping his promise to save us

I don't suppose my life will ever be 'normal' now

This week's prayer

My soul glorifies the Lord and my Spirit rejoices in God my saviour. Amen

Z E I E T B A L H

Mary met ☐☐☐☐☐☐☐☐☐, her cousin.

They were very happy about what God was doing.

Draw them here

CHRISTMAS

CHRISTMAS DAY

Thought for the day

Emmanuel – 'God with us' – is born at Bethlehem into the human family. Now we will be able to understand, in human terms, what God is really like.

Readings

Isaiah 9:2-7
Psalm 96
Titus 2:11-14
Luke 2:1-14 (15-20)

Activities

Christmas Day is very much a time for all God's children to worship together.

Involve all the children in the singing and playing of carols, decorating the church, and in the other ministries of welcoming, serving, collection of gifts and so on.

I have included a drawing and colouring activity for today so that children in church can work at this during the sermon.

Notes

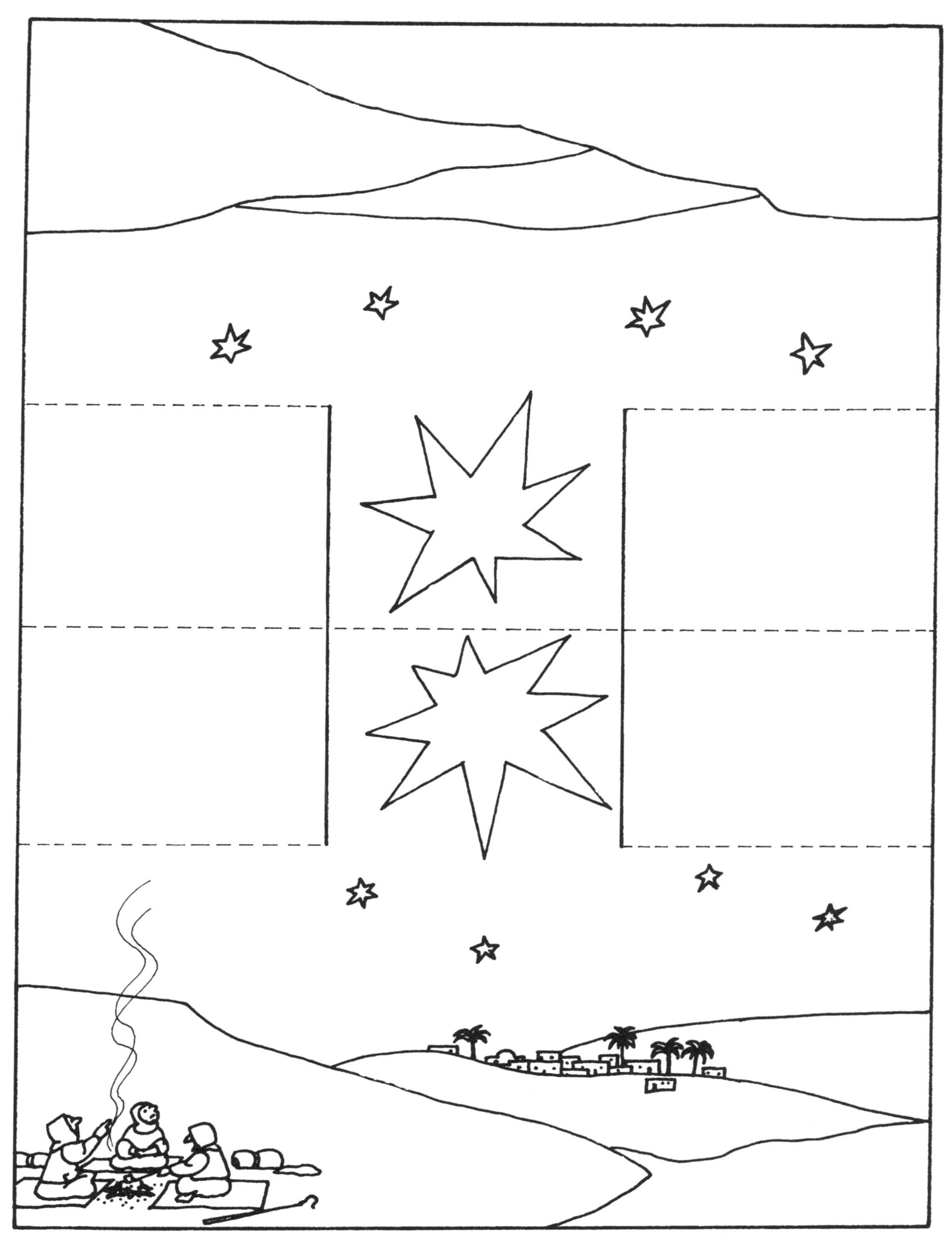

Colour, cut out and fold.
Stand on the table for Christmas dinner.

First Sunday of Christmas

Thought for the day

Jesus' perception and understanding of his purpose and work begins to take shape throughout his childhood.

Readings

1 Samuel 2:18-20, 26
Psalm 148
Colossians 3:12-17
Luke 2:41-52

Aim

To understand that Jesus shared a human childhood, and to look at the kind of experiences he would probably have had.

Starter

Sit in a circle and pass round a toy as each person has a turn to speak. Only the one holding the toy can speak. The first round is 'What I liked best about this Christmas was . . .' Anyone not wanting to speak just passes the toy on. The next round is 'The job I hate having to do is . . .'

Teaching

Have a timeline displayed to help the children place Jesus' birth in its historical context. (Copy this from the timeline drawn on the worksheet.) Have available some library books, travel brochures and Bibles with pictures of Palestine under the Romans and some photographs of the country surrounding Bethlehem. Have a large flat stone or board to demonstrate grinding flour and kneading dough, and a display of some of the raisins and dates and nuts that would have been grown and eaten.

Give the children a 'living museum' experience of what life would have been like for Jesus and his friends, bringing in whatever examples and artefacts you can get hold of. You may for instance be able to borrow some fabric or traditional clothing from the area, or traditional lamps or bedrolls, or you could use the pictures. The more involved the children are the better.

They can find out about sitting crosslegged on the floor and chanting from memory in school, and the kind of local jobs that would be the equivalent of a paper round, such as sheep watching, or helping with the harvest.

Praying

Jesus, you know what it's like
to be the same age as me.
Remind me that I can
talk things over with you
whenever I want
and you always
have time to listen. Amen.

Activities

Use the worksheet to consolidate the teaching, looking at the different areas of life for children in Jesus' time and comparing and contrasting with their own lives. There are suggestions for making a display to put up in church.

Notes

2000 Abraham lived — 1500 built in Egypt — 1000 King David lived — 500 Greeks ruled — Romans ruled — 0 Jesus lived — Romans left Britain — 500 — 1000 Battle of Hastings — 1500 Columbus sailed to America — 2000 You live

Jesus grows up

Make a display. Colour enlarged letters from a spare sheet for the title. You will need pictures drawn of

- a house in Nazareth
- a village well
- a palm tree
- bread making
- a map showing Nazareth
- children in school
- a water jug
- a child with sheep

Write about each picture. Stick everything on a large sheet of paper.

Jesus and I both . . .

drink water
go to school
learn things by heart
play with our friends
ride bikes
eat bread
get thirsty
pick fruit
walk to school
visit the family
help at home
get hungry
make our bed
watch the sun set
fetch water home
look after animals

Circle the things you both do.

Draw Jesus at school or helping Mum or Dad at home or playing.

This week's prayer

Jesus, you know what it's like to be the same age as me. Remind me that I can talk things over with you whenever I want and you always have time to listen. Amen.

Second Sunday of Christmas

Thought for the day

Christ is the way God tells people about himself.

Readings

Jeremiah 31:7-14
Psalm 147:12-20
Ephesians 1:3-14
John 1:(1-9) 10-18

Aim

To see Jesus as the Word of God.

Starter

Sit in a circle. Name the children in order round the circle: apple, orange, banana. Remove one chair and stand in the middle. Call 'banana!' and all the bananas get up and change places, while the person in the centre is trying to get a vacated seat. Whoever is left in the middle calls the next fruit, and so on. If the person in the middle calls 'fruit salad!' then everyone changes places.

Teaching

Draw attention to the way that in the game the person in the middle made certain things happen by the word they spoke. What other words in our language set things happening? (Words like 'Silence!' and 'Help!' and 'Quick march!') What word was spoken by God to start our world being made? ('Let there be light.' They can look it up in Genesis 1 and on the worksheet.) Read the first three verses of John 1 so that they can see how important God's word, or message, or communication was. If you have these displayed, the older children and better readers will be able to read it together. Or the children can repeat it after you, line by line.

Now read part of today's Gospel, starting at verse 14, asking the children to listen out for the word 'Word', and try and work out who it means. How can God's Word be in the world?

If they have no idea, remind them that the Word spoken by God at creation was God expressing his love. What person can they think of who expresses God's love, or tells us about God's love? If possible, draw the children to see for themselves that Jesus is the Word of God, rather than telling them outright. All words have power, and God's Word of love is not just sounds, but a person. Jesus is God saying 'I love you!'

Praying

Jesus, you are the loving Word of God.
Speak in my life
and help me to listen. Amen.

Activities

The power of words is looked at on the worksheet, and this leads on to reinforce John's teaching of Jesus expressing God's love in human terms we can understand. Instructions are given for creating a banner on this truth which can be carried into church and displayed for the benefit of the rest of the community.

Notes

God's Word of love

How do these words make you feel?

And God said,
'Let there be LIGHT!'
And there was light.

Genesis 1

In the beginning
was the Word,
and the Word was with God
and the Word was God.
He was with God
in the beginning and
through him all things were
made.

John 1

I think the Word is . . .

How to make a banner.
You will need:

* large sheet of paper
* rod * coloured paper
* string * templates
* scissors * glue

1 Plan your design
2 Cut and stick to make it up
3 Cut the banner as above
4 Stick it down over the rod
5 Tie string on the rod

IDEAS

You want to show people that Jesus is God saying 'I love you'.
With a friend think of letters or pictures to show this.
Try them out!

This week's prayer:

Jesus, you are the loving Word of God. Speak in my life and help me to listen.

Amen.

EPIPHANY

THE EPIPHANY

Thought for the day

Jesus, the hope of the nations, is shown to the world.

Readings

Isaiah 60:1-6
Psalm 72:(1-9) 10-15
Ephesians 3:1-12
Matthew 2:1-12

Aim

To explore why the wise men made their journey and what they found out.

Starter

Who am I? Fix a picture of an animal or food item on everyone's back. They have to find out who they are by going round asking questions about themselves. The others can only answer yes or no.

Teaching

Point out how in the game they had to search for the right answer, and it was like a journey to find the truth. Sometimes people were helpful in that and sometimes they weren't. Today we are looking at some wise men who set out on a quest.

Have two or three adults meeting up as if they are resting on the journey and chatting together about what the day has been like, what they miss, and what they are hoping to find. It is best to try out the conversation beforehand but without any set words as it will then sound natural.

When the wise men have settled down for the night (or gone to feed the camels), show the children a sheet of paper with these headings on it: Who? What? Why? In the different sections brainstorm ideas about who they were (wise men from the East), what they were doing (following a star to find a baby king of great importance) and why they bothered (they had worked out from the signs that this birth was really important for the human race, and they felt a strong urge to be there and pay their respects). Use the children's words, of course.

Now have the wise men on their way back, talking about how they felt about King Herod, what it was like to see Jesus, and why they are going home by a different route.

Praying

Have some incense, gold and myrrh on display during the teaching. As each is brought to the front pray together:

Gold
The wise men brought gold to Jesus.
Jesus, we bring you the gold of our obedience.
Help us to live as you want us to. Amen.

Frankincense
The wise men brought frankincense to Jesus.
Jesus, we bring you the incense of our worship.
You are God and we worship you. Amen.

Myrrh
The wise men brought myrrh to Jesus.
Jesus, we bring you the myrrh of the world's sadness.
Help us to look after one another better. Amen.

Activities

You will need lots of lining paper or rolls of wallpaper. The best present we can give to Jesus is ourselves. Working in twos, the children draw round each other on the paper, cut themselves out and colour them. On the front write:

Jesus,
the best present
I can give you
is myself!

The cut-outs can be offered with the gifts in church and given back at the end of the service for the children to remember at home.

The worksheet has a sequencing activity to consolidate the teaching, and a look at our own journey to Jesus.

Notes

Colour these pictures, cut them out and stick them in the right order . . .

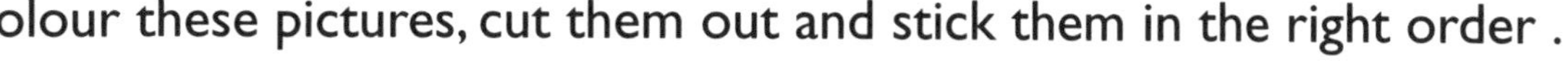

The wise men come to see Jesus

over here

Where are you on your journey to find Jesus? Have you found him yet? Draw in yourself where you feel you are.

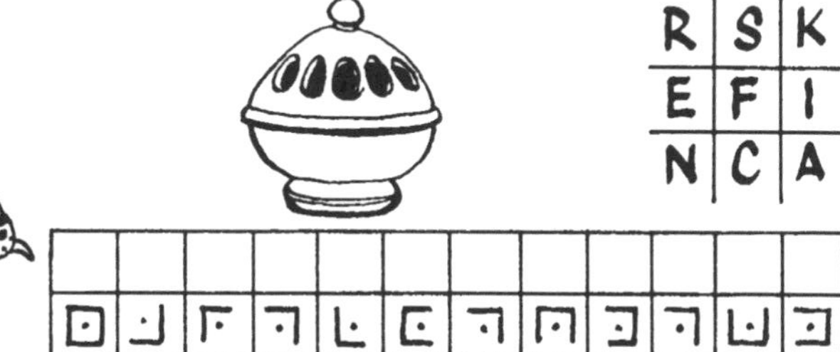

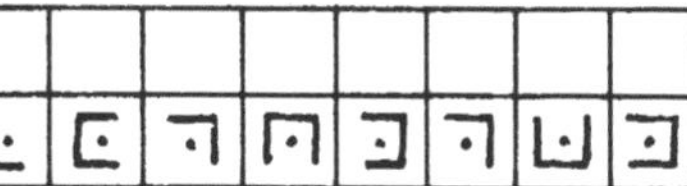

R	S	K
E	F	I
N	C	A

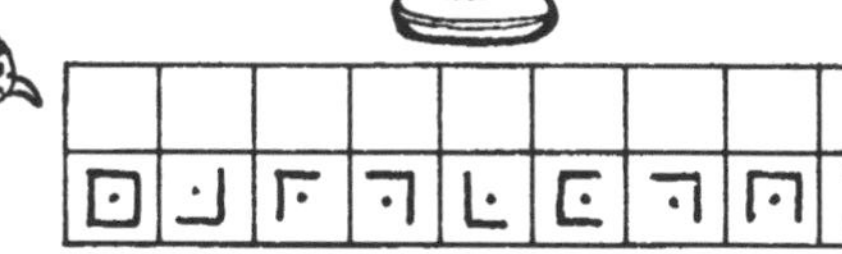

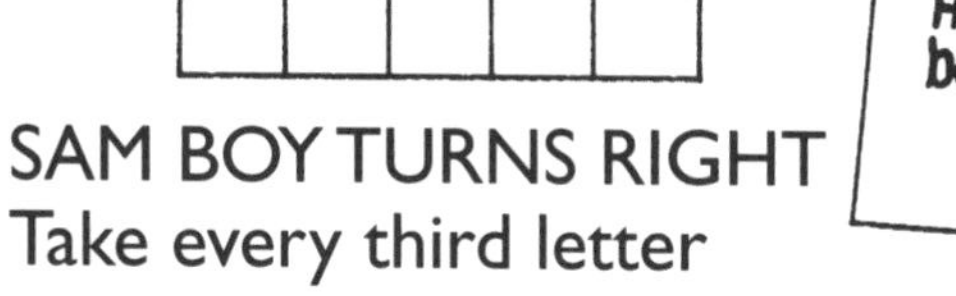

SAM BOY TURNS RIGHT
Take every third letter

This week's prayer

GOLD
We bring you the gold of our obedience.
Help us live as you want us to.

FRANKINCENSE
We bring you the incense of our worship.
You are God and we worship you.

MYRRH
We bring you the myrrh of our world's sadness.
Help us look after one another better.

Amen.

The Baptism of Christ: First Sunday of Epiphany

Thought for the day

Jesus is baptised, and God confirms his identity and his calling.

Readings

Isaiah 43:1-7
Psalm 29
Acts 8:14-17
Luke 3:15-17, 21-22

Aim

To get to know the story of Jesus' Baptism according to Luke.

Starter

Show pictures of famous people and characters in books, and see how many everyone can identify. Or you could match names with pictures.

Teaching

Bring along some Baptism certificates (a mixture of old and recent ones) and any other signs of Baptism that your church or the children's families have, such as Christening robes, special candles, cards and presents to mark the occasion. It is a very special and important day for us because when we are christened or baptised with water in the name of God the Father, Son and Holy Spirit, we are called by name to follow Jesus, and we decide to follow the Christian way of life.

Today we are going to look at what happened when Jesus was baptised in the River Jordan. Spread out the carpet tiles, or ground- and sky-coloured sheets or towels, with a blue river of paper or material running through the landscape. Base your pictures on the ones on the sheet. Put John the Baptist standing in the water, calling the people to make their lives clean, ready for the coming of the Messiah or Christ. Put in the crowds of people listening to him and deciding to put their lives right. Put in some people in the water and move John the Baptist around baptising them.

There was someone there that day who didn't need to clean up his life at all. It was Jesus. (Put him in.) He came with all the other people because he loved them and wanted to show that he was with them. We don't know what Jesus was praying as he went into the water and was baptised, but we do know that when he had been baptised he was filled with the Holy Spirit. It seemed like a pure white dove flying out of heaven to rest gently on him. (Place the dove just above Jesus.) God's voice was heard from heaven, saying to him, 'You are my Son and I love you; I am very pleased with you.'

In a way, Jesus was being told his name. He was being told who he was, and what he was called to be during his time on earth.

Praying

Dear Jesus,
you know me even better
than I know myself.
Help me to grow in your Spirit
day by day, all my life through,
rich with the gift of your love. Amen.

Activities

There are instructions on the sheet for making a model of the Baptism of Jesus. Each child will need a shoe box, cotton, card, colouring pens and glue.

Notes

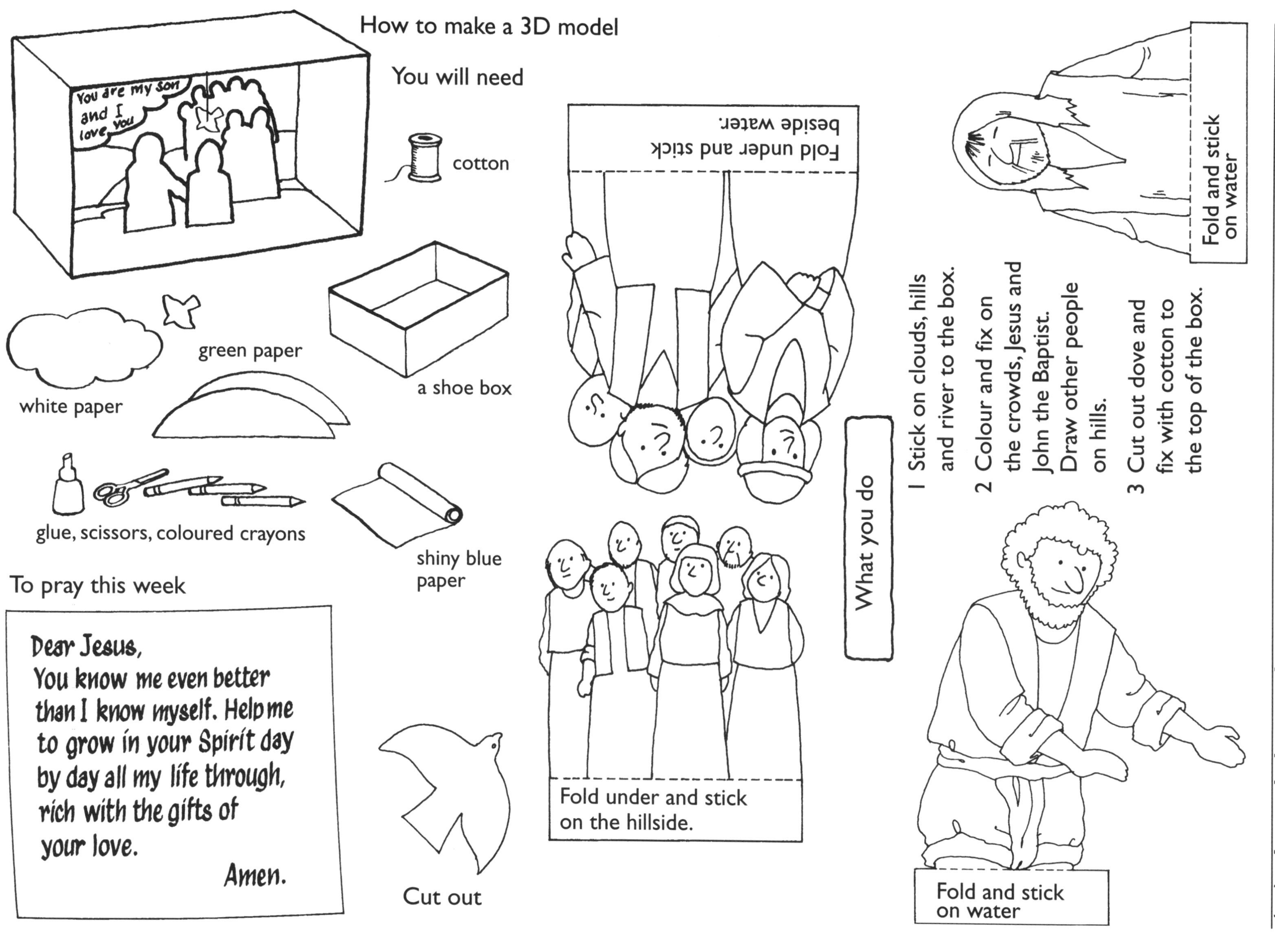

How to make a 3D model
You are my Son and I love you
You will need
cotton
a shoe box
white paper
green paper
glue, scissors, coloured crayons
shiny blue paper
To pray this week
Dear Jesus,
You know me even better than I know myself. Help me to grow in your Spirit day by day all my life through, rich with the gifts of your love.
Amen.
Cut out
Fold under and stick beside water.
Fold under and stick on the hillside.
What you do
1 Stick on clouds, hills and river to the box.
2 Colour and fix on the crowds, Jesus and John the Baptist. Draw other people on hills.
3 Cut out dove and fix with cotton to the top of the box.
Fold and stick on water
Fold and stick on water

Second Sunday of Epiphany

Thought for the day

As a marriage celebrates the beginning of a changed, new life for the bride and groom, so our loving, faithful God has chosen us and is ready to transform our lives for the good of the world.

Readings

Isaiah 62:1-5
Psalm 36:5-10
1 Corinthians 12:1-11
John 2:1-11

Aim

To see the wedding at Cana as a sign of God's glory shown in Jesus.

Starter

A tasting survey. Have a number of different fruit drinks and some drinking cups. Blindfold some volunteers and give them the different drinks to taste, asking them to name them. Record their opinions on a chart and then let them take off the blindfold and reveal the identity of the drinks.

Teaching

Explain how we are going to hear about some people whose drink gave them a rather nice surprise. Have one of the servants telling the story. S/he can be holding a water jar and wearing appropriate clothing or headcovering to add to the effect. Whoever is telling the story needs to know the events well, and see it all from the servant's point of view. You can then slip in bits of hearsay about this man, Jesus, and comment on how you felt as he told you what to say and what it was that made you prepared to go along with what he told you to do. The aim is to help the children see what happened as if they were there as well.

Remind the children of the meaning of epiphany, and talk over with them what was being shown about God in this event. Read what John says at the end of his account. They had already decided to follow, and this sign backed up their decision.

Praying

Fill us up to the brim
with your Spirit, O Lord,

with hands horizontal like a water level, raise the level to the top of your head

and use our lives

open up hands and extend them in offering

for the good of the world.

trace large circle in the air with hands

Amen.

Activities

The teaching is reinforced on the worksheet with an activity which matches different people with different reactions. There is also space to record discussion outcomes concerning the significance of this event. Instructions are included for making a 'black-and-white into colour' picture.

Notes

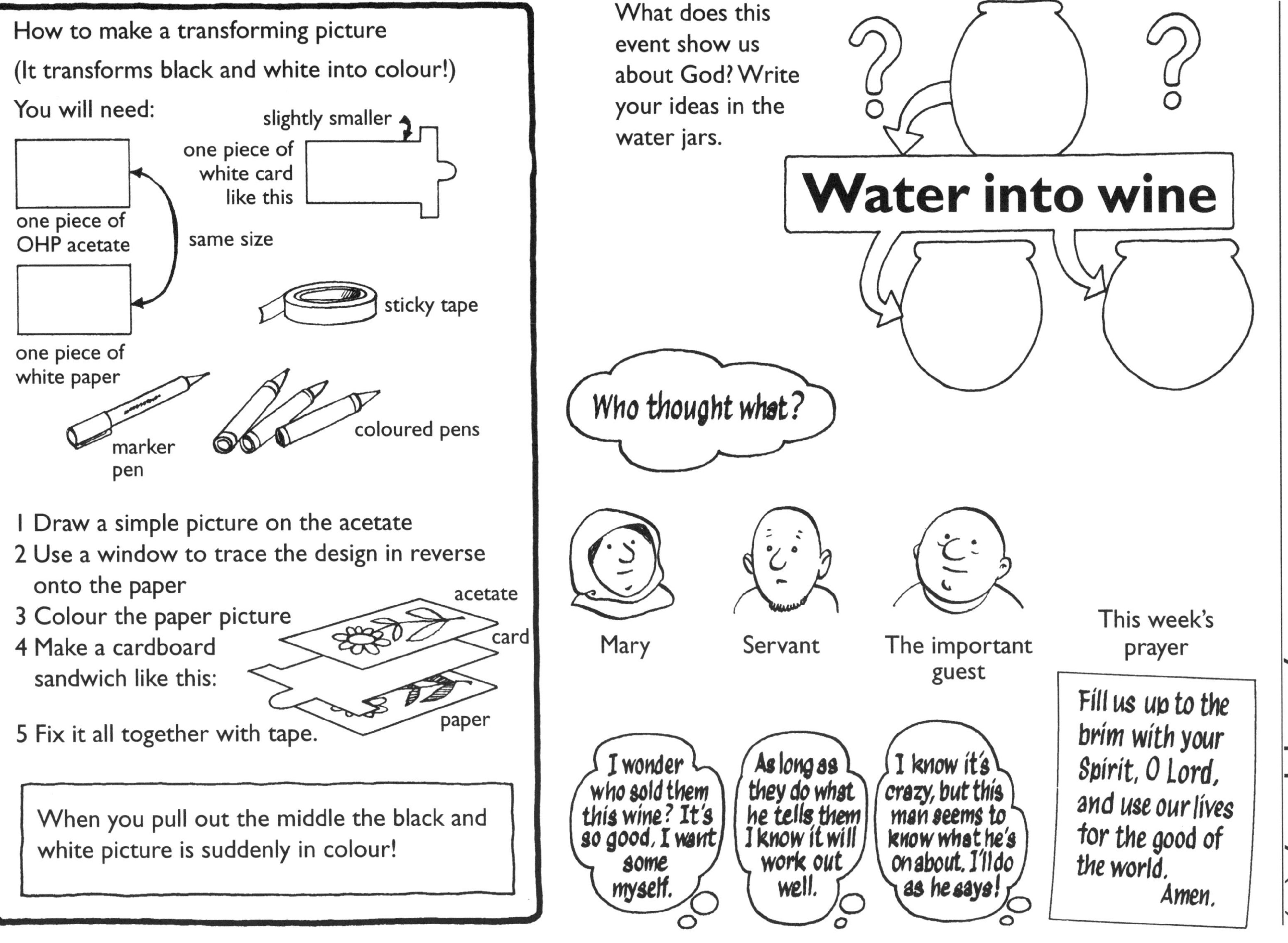
How to make a transforming picture
(It transforms black and white into colour!)
You will need:
one piece of OHP acetate
same size
one piece of white paper
slightly smaller
one piece of white card like this
sticky tape
marker pen
coloured pens
1 Draw a simple picture on the acetate
2 Use a window to trace the design in reverse onto the paper
3 Colour the paper picture
4 Make a cardboard sandwich like this:
acetate
card
paper
5 Fix it all together with tape.
When you pull out the middle the black and white picture is suddenly in colour!
What does this event show us about God? Write your ideas in the water jars.
Water into wine
Who thought what?
Mary
Servant
The important guest
I wonder who sold them this wine? It's so good, I want some myself.
As long as they do what he tells them I know it will work out well.
I know it's crazy, but this man seems to know what he's on about. I'll do as he says!
This week's prayer
Fill us up to the brim with your Spirit, O Lord, and use our lives for the good of the world. Amen.

THIRD SUNDAY OF EPIPHANY

Thought for the day

The meaning of the scriptures is revealed to the people.

Readings

Nehemiah 8:1-3, 5-6, 8-10
Psalm 19
1 Corinthians 12:12-31a
Luke 4:14-21

Aim

To see how God is revealed through the scriptures.

Starter

Who can it be? Sit in a circle. Start giving one piece of information about a particular child and continue down the clues until someone guesses who you are describing.

Teaching

Point out how in the game the words that were spoken gave everyone clues about the person being described. No one has ever seen God in this life, but we have been given plenty of good clues in the writings in the Bible. Look together at the passage from Isaiah. Who do they think it sounds as if it is describing? It does sound very like Jesus because he did those things in his life.

This prophecy of Isaiah was well known to the people in the town of Nazareth, where Jesus grew up. But at that time they had no idea who the prophet was talking about. They were in for quite a surprise one morning when they went to worship at their local synagogue.

Now act out the Gospel by having it fixed on a scroll. Read the first section from the Bible. An attendant then hands you a scroll from which you read verses 17b to 20a. Hand back the scroll and continue reading from the Bible. Make yourself thoroughly familiar with the text beforehand so that the other parts of the Gospel can be told informally. Have the words of the chorus to *God's Spirit is in my heart* displayed so that they can be read or sung afterwards:

> He sent me to give the Good News to the poor
> tell pris'ners that they are pris'ners no more,
> tell blind people that they can see
> and set the downtrodden free,
> and go tell ev'ryone
> the news that the kingdom of God has come
> and go tell ev'ryone
> the news that God's kingdom has come.

Talk together about how they might have felt if they had been there that morning and record their ideas on a sheet of paper headed: 'When Jesus preached this week I wondered/felt/thought . . .'. Then you can write their thoughts in thought bubbles.

Praying

Jesus, I know you always speak what is true.
Help me to listen
with my heart as well as my ears. Amen.

Activities

Make a group collage of today's Gospel, based on the picture drawn below. Give the children the appropriate sized pieces of paper to draw various people from the town and clothe them by cutting and sticking from a selection of different coloured and textured paper or fabric. All the characters are then assembled in the synagogue and Jesus can be holding a rolled scroll. The title for the collage is 'Today this scripture is fulfilled in your hearing'.

The worksheet looks at our need to listen so that when God is speaking to us through his word we are able to hear him.

Notes

How loud?

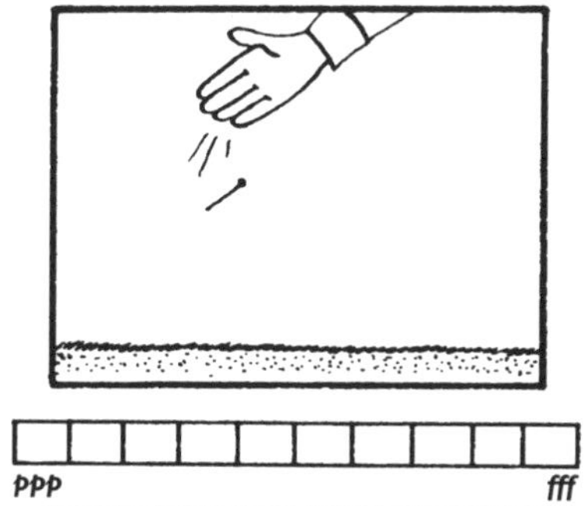

ppp fff

ppp fff

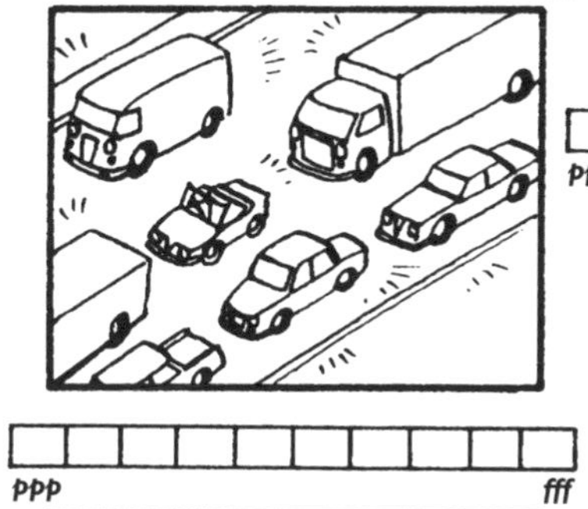

ppp fff

ppp fff

ppp fff

Mark it on the scale

We can hear some things easily.
To hear others we have to listen
very carefully.

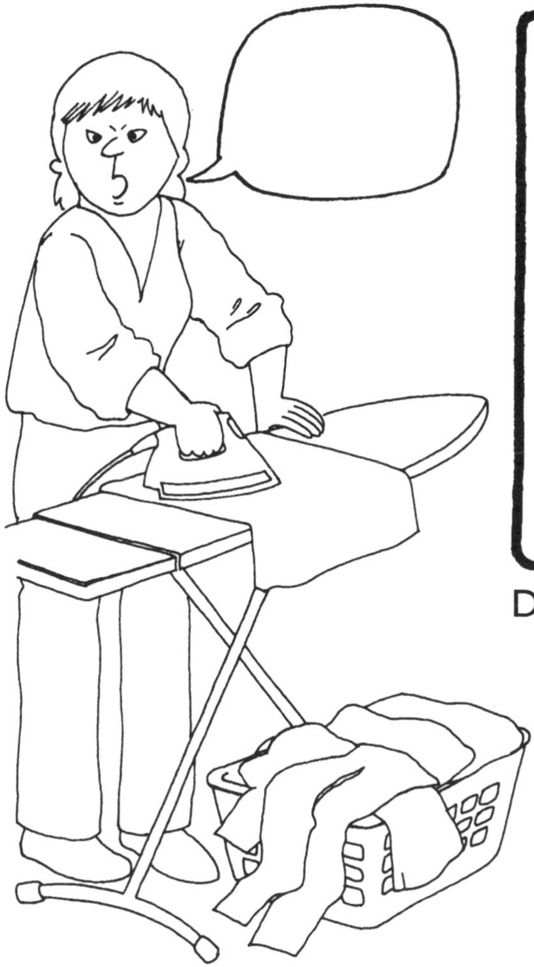

What might you pretend
not to hear Mum say?
(next time, listen and hear!)

Draw a person for a synagogue collage

This week's prayer

Jesus,
I know you always
speak what is true.
Help me to listen
with my heart as
well as my ears.
Amen.

When do we need to listen
to what God is saying?

FOURTH SUNDAY OF EPIPHANY

Thought for the day

At eight days old, Jesus is presented in the temple, and at the Purification is revealed to Simeon and Anna as the promised Saviour who is able to reveal to us our true selves.

Readings

Ezekiel 43:27-44:4
Psalm 48
1 Corinthians 13:1-13
Luke 2:22-40

Aim

To see that Jesus was being shown to those who were close to God and wanted to see.

Starter

Piecing the story together. Have a large-scale floor jigsaw and give the pieces out to everyone in the circle. One person starts by putting down their piece, and then you go round the circle adding pieces bit by bit until the picture is complete. This may well mean that some people can't go until someone else has added another piece. All through the season of Epiphany we have been looking at Jesus being shown to the world. All the different stories come together to give us a clearer picture of who he is and why he came.

Teaching

Have Anna and Simeon chatting together in the temple after Jesus has been taken home. They are talking about what has happened, and how they knew this particular baby was the promised Messiah. The children are listening in to the conversation. In the conversation bring out their age and their hopes, the way God has shown them the Saviour and their joy at recognising him. After the story get out two sheets, headed 'Simeon' and 'Anna'. Build a factfile about the two people we have just met, under the following headings:

Age Group (Young / Middle aged / Old)

Prayer Life (Prayed from time to time / Prayed if they felt like it / Close friendship with God)

Hope (The Messiah coming / Meeting the Messiah / Recognising the Messiah)

What they thought of Jesus (A cute baby / An ordinary baby / The promised Messiah)

Praying

Simeon's prayer of praise. This translation from the *International Children's Bible* is a suitable one to use:

Now, Lord, you can let me, your servant,
die in peace as you said.
I have seen your Salvation with my own eyes.
It is Jesus.
You prepared him before all people.
He is a light for the non-Jewish people to see.
He is the glory of your chosen people.
I believe that Jesus is my Lord and Saviour.

Say it line by line with the children repeating.

Activities

The worksheet extends the teaching to include what Simeon foretold about Jesus and his ministry. There are also instructions for making a prayer diary for the children to develop their own prayer life.

Notes

Name
Age group
Prayer life
Hope
What he thinks of Jesus
Name
Age group
Prayer life
Hope
What she thinks of Jesus
He will be...
He will...
What Simeon said about Jesus
Some people...
He will have to... and
How to make a prayer diary
You will need: some A4 paper/an A4 sheet of wrapping paper/an A4 piece of card/a punch/a length of string or wool
Date
Prayers
How God answered
Don't forget – Prayers can ASK, THANK, PRAISE, SAY SORRY, TALK OVER WORRIES, LISTEN OR JUST ENJOY GOD'S COMPANY
This week's prayer
I have seen your Salvation with my own eyes.
It is Jesus.
You prepared him before all people.
He is a light for the non-Jewish people to see.
He is the glory of your chosen people.
I believe that Jesus is my Lord and Saviour.
Amen.

ORDINARY TIME

Proper 1

Sunday between 3 and 9 February inclusive
(if earlier than the Second Sunday before Lent)

Thought for the day

God calls his people and commissions them.

Readings

Isaiah 6:1-8 (9-13)
Psalm 138
1 Corinthians 15:1-11
Luke 5:1-11

Aim

To see the stages that Simon Peter went through in this calling.

Starter

Pass it on. Sit in a circle and choose a leader. The leader does something (claps hands, crosses legs, winks, etc.) and this action is taken up by each person one by one, going clockwise round the circle. When it gets back to the leader, they start a new action for the next round. The point is that each person needs to be attentive to what the person sitting next to them is doing, and they then become the next in the chain of passing the message on.

Teaching

Beforehand prepare a film clapperboard to snap shut as signs with the following headings are displayed. (The titles in brackets are written on the reverse.)

1. The night shift
2. Simon helps out *(welcome Jesus)*
3. Time to listen *(listen to him)*
4. The Maker's instructions *(see him in action)*
5. I'm not good enough! *(recognise who he is)*
6. Follow me *(follow him)*

Go through the story as if the film is being made, narrating it, with the leaders and children acting it out.

1. The children act the setting-out and pulling-in of empty nets through the night.
2. The crowd arrives, and Simon Peter offers Jesus his boat to sit in.
3. Simon Peter sits on the sand with the crowd, first busy with his nets and gradually listening more keenly. Give out an old net curtain for everyone to work on.
4. Jesus tells the fishermen to cast their nets again and they do so, with surprising and dramatic results.
5. Simon Peter reacts to the huge catch by realising Jesus' importance and his own lack of goodness.
6. Jesus shows Simon Peter that he knows what he is like and still wants him to work for the spreading of the kingdom of God. He calls him to follow and search for people instead of fish. Simon Peter follows him.

Display all the signs in order, then turn them over to show the titles in brackets. These lead on to the prayer time.

Praying

Give the children a set of five paper footprints, which they put down in a line in front of them. As you pray, move forward to each footprint in turn:

Like Simon Peter
I want to *welcome* you, Jesus,
listen to what you say,
see what you do,
get to *know* you better
and *follow* you all my life. Amen.

Activities

On the sheet there are instructions for making a fishes-and-shell mobile, based on today's prayer. You will need to have string, card, and a shell for each child. There is also a wordsearch to reinforce the teaching, and a picture to complete, which will give them the sense of things falling into place as Jesus enables us to see where we need to go next in life.

Notes

Word Search

F	A	J	O	T	H	E	R	W	P
S	I	E	A	B	Q	D	U	M	T
I	T	S	P	C	A	T	C	H	O
M	E	U	H	S	C	Y	G	E	N
O	B	S	C	I	R	I	C	N	S
N	P	U	Z	G	N	B	O	A	T
I	F	A	L	S	H	G	L	V	E
A	N	Y	T	H	I	N	G	D	N
J	H	O	I	X	E	J	F	M	O
K	L	G	L	K	P	E	T	E	R

SIMON PETER went FISHING all NIGHT but he didn't CATCH ANYTHING. JESUS told him to let down the NETS on the OTHER side of the BOAT. This time they caught LOTS of fish.

How to make a fish mobile

You will need:
some string and a shell
6 fish

1. Colour the fish and cut them out
2. Thread them on to the string with a knot below each fish so it won't slip
3. Stick a shell to the bottom of the string
4. Make a loop at the top
5. Hang it up and pray it

Like Simon Peter...

I want to WELCOME you Jesus...

LISTEN to what you say...

SEE what you do...

GET TO KNOW YOU better...

and FOLLOW YOU all my life.

PROPER 2

Sunday between 10 and 6 February inclusive
(if earlier than the Second Sunday before Lent)

Thought for the day

The challenges and rewards of living by faith.

Readings

Jeremiah 17:5-10
Psalm 1
1 Corinthians 15:12-20
Luke 6:17-26

Aim

To think about where we put our trust, and whether this is the best place for it.

Starter

See I haven't got it! Use a soft ball or beanbag. The children line up across one end of the room and a child at the other end throws the ball into the centre of the room before turning away from the other children. The children run to collect the ball and whoever has it tries not to show it. The child who threw the ball can ask anyone to turn round and eventually guesses who has it.

Teaching

First refer to the starter game. Ask the children who were trying to decide who had the ball, if they felt they could trust those who said they hadn't got it. (No, they couldn't trust them because the game meant they were hiding the truth.) What or whom can we trust? Today we are going to look at some teaching of Jesus. He was helping people see what they really trusted in.

(Use the carpet tiles method to tell the story. Pictures needed are shown below.)

Luke tells us that Jesus had been on a mountain-side praying all night long before choosing his twelve apostles. They had all agreed to leave their homes and jobs and set out with Jesus. That was a big thing to do, and a lot to give up. Ask the children what might have worried the apostles about their new life and give them some ideas. (Will there be enough to eat? Where will we sleep? Will people think I am stupid? Am I being stupid? Will it be dangerous? Will I be able to do it well enough?)

Jesus brought the apostles to a large level place, and lots of people came to hear what he said. Some of these people were his friends and followers, and some were people who didn't want to follow him because that would mean changing the way they lived and they were comfortable as they were.

First Jesus spoke to the ones who had given up their security to follow him. He told them that the choice they had made – to risk being poor and hungry and sad and insulted, in order to do what was right and good – was a choice that would bring them great rewards of happiness, happiness that would last for ever.

Then he spoke to those who still put all their trust in being rich and having lots of possessions, and doing only what would keep them popular. He told them that we can't get long-term happiness and security from things other people say and make and sell. This kind of richness doesn't last and will leave us poor in the end because it will make us greedy and selfish and never satisfied.

Praying

There is a real challenge to people of all ages in today's teaching, and it is important that we never force children to make decisions or feel they have to believe things they are not ready to. At the same time, it is very important that we give them all the opportunity to voice their love and commitment. Invite the children to join in this prayer having read it to them first. If they don't feel ready to pray it they needn't. Ask them simply to sit quietly so they allow others to pray.

Lord God,
I want to live by faith in you.
I understand that it may not be easy,
but I can see it is the best way to live.
Please show me how.
Thank you. Amen.

Activities

On the worksheet there are instructions for making a contrasting collage of living rooted in God and rooted in a dry place. The children also explore trust at different levels so they can begin to see the difference between enjoying what God has provided, and becoming so attached to something that it takes over our life and stops us moving on.

1 Cover both sides of an old card with blue paper
2 For (a) cut out sandpaper and stick on. Stick on a yellow sun and a dead twig.
3 For (b) stick on shiny blue water and green grass. Cut out the brown tree trunk, green leaves and red fruit. Stick them on the background.
4 Cut out this week's prayer and stick it on (b).
5 Stand your collage where you need to be reminded.

This week's prayer

> Lord God,
> I want to live by faith in you. I understand that it may not be easy, but I can see it is the best way to live.
> Please show me how.
> Thank you.
> Amen.

Which of these do you enjoy? Put a ring round them.

Thank you, God, for all these good things.

Jeremiah 17:7

the who like water a be be planted will blessed. trusts He the tree The Lord in person near strong. will

but . . .

What if one of these stops you

- helping at home
- sharing
- going to church
- being kind

?

Help me get it right, God

PROPER 3

Sunday between 17 and 23 February inclusive
(if earlier than the Second Sunday before Lent)

Thought for the day

Jesus teaches us to love our enemies and forgive those who sin against us.

Readings

Genesis 45:3-11, 15
Psalm 37:1-11, 39-40
1 Corinthians 15:35-38, 42-50
Luke 6:27-38

Aim

To explore what it means to love enemies.

Starter

Play any quick softball or beanbag game in two teams, so they experience working against one another. In all these games each side is trying to make it hard for the other. Point out that in the game we are playing at being enemies.

Teaching

Sit everyone in a circle and pass a card round with the word 'enemies' on it. As each person holds the card they say, 'An enemy is someone who . . .' If they don't wish to say anything they just pass the card on. The rule is that only the person holding the card can speak.

Draw all the ideas together, or record them on paper. Then place a card which says 'Love your' in front of the other card so they can see Jesus' teaching: Love your enemies. Surely that can't be right? We've just heard all these nasty things about enemies, and here is Jesus telling us to love them. How on earth can we do that? How can we love someone who's always out to get us, and hates us?

Check in the Bible and find that it isn't a mistake; it really says, 'love your enemies'. Read the passage together.

Ask the children to make their faces full of hate and bitterness. Get them to notice how hard the muscles have to work to do it. It's better and healthier for us not to make a habit of hating and sulking if we're upset, and God knows that. Perhaps they can remember seeing some older people's faces. If we are always thinking life isn't fair, and we hate and resent people, it will show in our faces as we get older. But if we get used to forgiving quickly, and putting the resentment down, that will show in our faces instead. It's right and it's sensible to take Jesus' teaching seriously, even though it is hard to do.

Have the three words of the teaching written on three balloons and learn the teaching off by heart by saying it several times, popping one balloon each time.

Praying

Forgive us our trespasses
as we forgive those
who trespass against us. Amen.

Activities

On the worksheet there are instructions for making a card and envelope to give to someone with whom they need to make up or strengthen a good relationship. The teaching is also reinforced with a code activity.

Notes

This week's prayer

Forgive us our trespasses as we forgive those who trespass against us.

Amen.

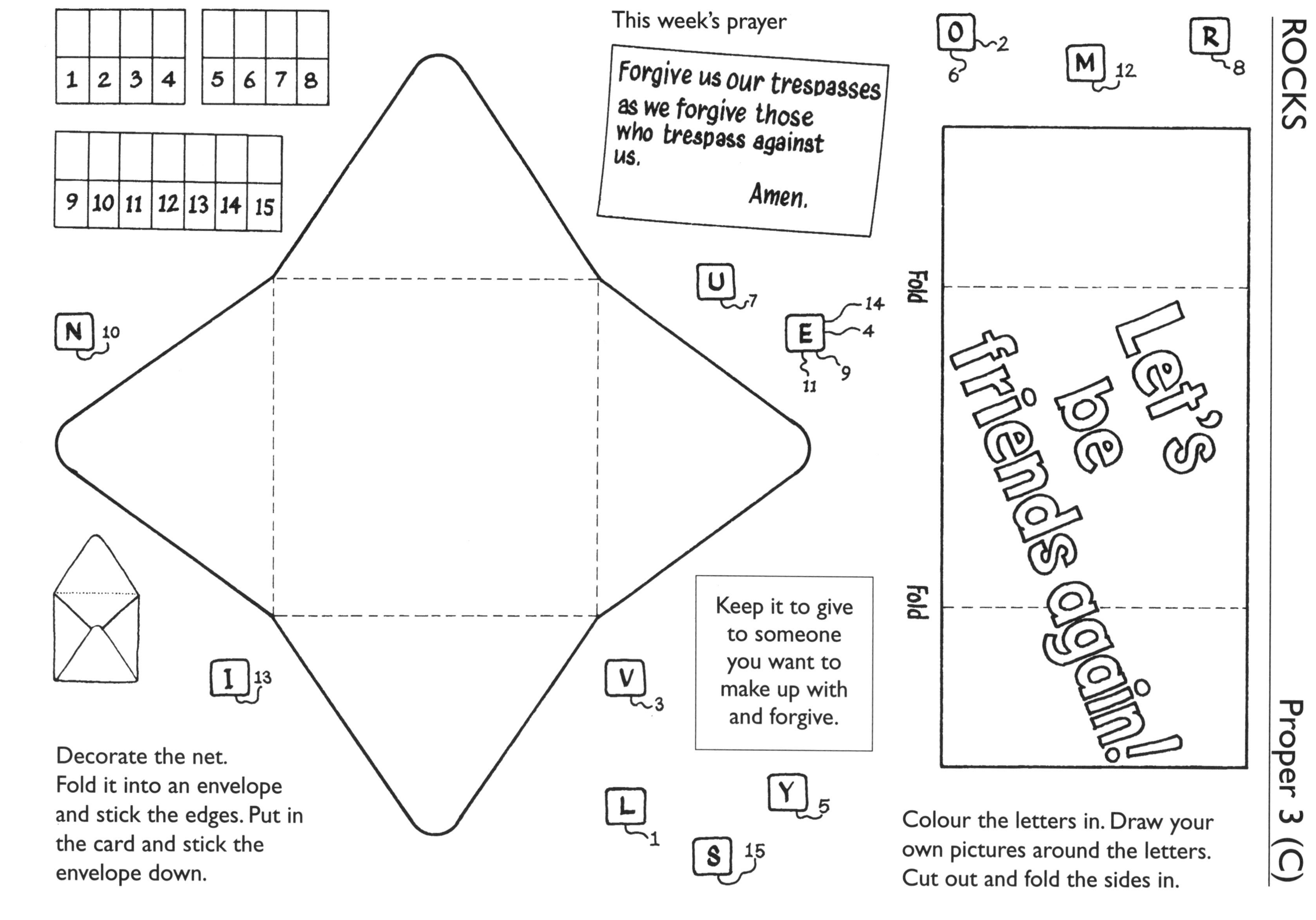

Keep it to give to someone you want to make up with and forgive.

Colour the letters in. Draw your own pictures around the letters. Cut out and fold the sides in.

Decorate the net.
Fold it into an envelope and stick the edges. Put in the card and stick the envelope down.

Second Sunday before Lent

Thought for the day

'He commands even the winds and the water and they obey him.'

Readings

Genesis 2:4b-9, 15-25
Psalm 65
Revelation 4
Luke 8:22-25

Aim

To get to know the story of Jesus calming the storm.

Starter

Simon says. This game picks up on the theme of authority – what Simon says goes!

Teaching

Point out that in the starter activity you don't follow anyone's commands except Simon's because Simon is the one 'in charge'.

Now get everyone to sit so that they make the sides of a boat, apart from Jesus and his friends, who wait outside. The boat people can also help make the sounds of the lapping water and the storm. Tell the story as the children act it out, climbing into the boat, setting sail, baling out water and waking the sleeping Jesus. If the boat sides sway together as the storm increases you get a very realistic sense of being in a rocking boat.

Talk about how the disciples must have felt when they saw Jesus asleep, and when he calmed the storm. Point out that Jesus is often known as the Word of God. It was the voice or words of God which had brought the whole world into being at the very start of things.

Praying

Lord God,
when Jesus spoke to the storm
it calmed down.
Please speak to me
when I am storming about
and calm me down as well. Amen.

Activities

The worksheet links the disciples' amazement at the calming of the storm with God's authority at creation. The children are led to see God's power and authority at work in Jesus. There are also instructions for making a boat which rocks about in the stormy water.

Notes

BOAT IN THE STORM

You will need:

a piece of card like this

with a slit cut beforehand

and a piece of card like this

a lolly stick

a boat shape made from card

and some glue

Paint or colour the waves blue, white and green, and the boat so it looks like wood.

Glue the lolly stick to the back of the boat like this:

And put the stick through the hole in the card like this:

Put some glue down the sides and stick the other bit of card on top.

Now you can move the boat along through the stormy sea.

❀	∝	❀	ϟ

☼	💧	❀

◇	◎	ϟ	☽

○	ϟ	☽

☼	💧	❀

👁	❀	○

∩	☆	❀	♣

💧	◎	⌂

Crack the code

A	B	D	E	H	I	M
○	☆	☽	❀	💧	◎	⌂
N	O	S	T	V	W	Y
ϟ	∩	👁	☼	∝	◇	♣

This week's prayer

Lord God,
When Jesus spoke to the storm it calmed down.
Please speak to me when I am storming about and calm me down as well.
Amen.

1. And God said: 'Let the waters be gathered in one place.'

God made the sea

2. Who made the sea?

Jesus said to the waves: 'Be still!'

3. Who must Jesus be?

Spot the link in 1
Think about 2
Fill in your own answer to 3

SUNDAY BEFORE LENT

Thought for the day

God's glory makes Moses' face radiant, and it transfigures Jesus as he prays on the mountain. Our lives, too, can become increasingly radiant as the Spirit transforms us.

Readings

Exodus 34:29-35
Psalm 99
2 Corinthians 3:12-4:2
Luke 9:28-36 (37-43)

Aim

To get to know the events of the Transfiguration.

Starter

Pass the smile; pass the frown. Sit in a circle. Someone starts by smiling at their neighbour who then passes the smile on around the group. When it gets back where it started, try passing the frown around the circle. For a real challenge, start a smile going in one direction and a frown in the other.

Teaching

Point out how the way we behave can get passed on to others. People who are happy often spread that around, and people who are gloomy and bad-tempered spread their gloom. The people who spent time with Jesus on earth were changed by being with him. Today we are going to hear two of those friends talking about a rather strange experience they had with Jesus, something they remembered for the rest of their lives.

Have two of the leaders (or two other volunteers imported for the occasion) being Peter and either James or John. You can have three people if resources run to this. They have just met up and are talking about what happened when they went up the mountain with Jesus and saw him shining as he prayed to his Father. Those who are chatting the story need to know the passage very well and talk it through together a couple of times beforehand. Think yourselves into character and talk about it as the real event it was, reminding one another of who you saw there, and what was said, thinking aloud your thoughts about what it meant, and why you were allowed to see it. The children will gain a great sense of immediacy if the conversation is informal but 'real'.

Have a mirror on the floor with several candles standing on it, and as the disciples get to the point when Jesus is deep in prayer have someone quietly lighting the candles. Nothing needs to be said about this, but the visual alongside the story will help touch their senses with understanding of the wonder of what was being seen.

Praying

Lord Jesus,
in your life we see the glory of God.
In our lives
we want to reflect God's glory
by the way we live.
May our lives
shine with love. Amen.

Activities

On the worksheet there are instructions for candle decorating. Great care must be taken to ensure everyone's safety. There is also a Bible study activity to reinforce the teaching and a picture to complete of the Transfiguration.

Notes

Candles

You will need:

a white candle

wax crayons

a night light in a tin foil dish

old newspapers

WHAT YOU DO

1 Protect your clothes, the table and the floor.

2 Peel the paper off the wax crayons.

3 Melt the end of a crayon and drip the wax onto the candle.

4 Use other colours and cover the candle with coloured wax blobs and trickles.

5 Light your candle each day while you pray this week's prayer.

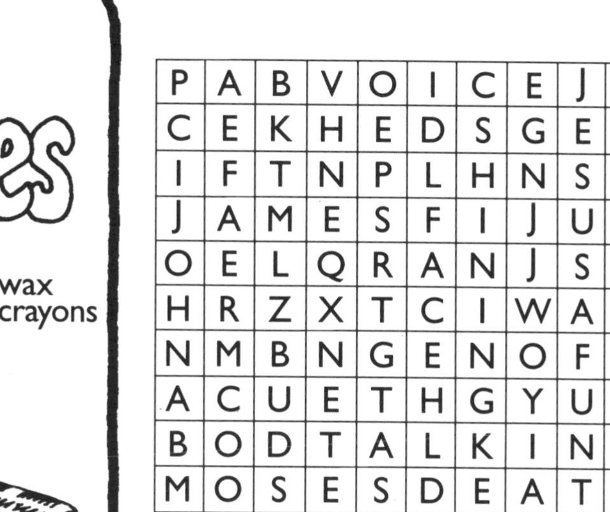

P	A	B	V	O	I	C	E	J	C
C	E	K	H	E	D	S	G	E	L
I	F	T	N	P	L	H	N	S	O
J	A	M	E	S	F	I	J	U	U
O	E	L	Q	R	A	N	J	S	D
H	R	Z	X	T	C	I	W	A	V
N	M	B	N	G	E	N	O	F	H
A	C	U	E	T	H	G	Y	U	K
B	O	D	T	A	L	K	I	N	G
M	O	S	E	S	D	E	A	T	H

JESUS took PETER, JAMES and JOHN up on a MOUNTAIN to pray. As Jesus prayed, his FACE and clothes started SHINING. Then there were two men TALKING with Jesus. They were MOSES and ELIJAH, and they were talking about Jesus' DEATH. Peter wanted it to last for ever. Then a CLOUD came down all around them and they heard God's VOICE saying, 'This is my S _ _, my ch _ _ _ _ one. Listen to him.' When the voice finished, Jesus was on his own with them again.
Luke 9:28-36

Draw in Jesus on the mountain talking to Moses and Elijah. Make Jesus look as if he is shining.

This week's prayer

Lord Jesus,
in your life
we see the glory of God.
In our lives
we want to reflect God's
glory by the way we live.
May our lives shine with
love. Amen.

LENT

First Sunday of Lent

Thought for the day

Following his Baptism, Jesus is severely tempted out in the desert, and shows us how to overcome temptation.

Readings

Deuteronomy 26:1-11
Psalm 91:1-2, 9-16
Romans 10:8b-13
Luke 4:1-13

Aim

To know the story of Jesus being tempted and overcoming the temptations.

Starter

Come and sit on my chair. Everyone stands behind a chair except one person who goes out of the room while everyone decides whose chair will be the 'correct' one. When the 'outsider' comes in, everyone tries to make her sit on their chair, and she chooses a seat. If it is the agreed one, the owner of that chair goes outside next. If the wrong chair is chosen she is (very gently) tipped off and can try again. If she gets it wrong three times, someone else goes out and another chair is agreed on.

Teaching

Talk about how we were all tempting our friends to sit on the wrong seat in the game. In real life we are often tempted to do what is wrong, and we sometimes tempt, or encourage, our friends and brothers and sisters to do what is wrong, or avoid doing what is right.

Straight after he was baptised, Jesus was badly tempted too, even before his work had properly begun. If he had given in to those temptations, we would not be here today.

First put a large stone down in the centre.

Jesus was very hungry. He was fasting, going without food, for forty days, as he talked over with God what his work was, and how it could be done. He knew that he could use God's power. Now he was tempted to use it, not to save people but to change the stones around him into bread so he could eat something.

He knew that would be a wrong way of using God's power. So he said to Satan, 'People don't just need real bread to live on – they need my Father's words to live on as well.' Jesus stuck with what was right, so he could go on to feed us with his Father's words of hope and truth.

Now put down a globe.

Satan showed Jesus all the countries of the world, and pretended that he could give them all to him straight away, if Jesus would just worship him. Jesus knew that would be completely wrong, and was a lie, so he told Satan that God is the one you worship, and no one else, no matter what they offer you.

Now put down a first aid box.

Satan suggested that he could win people to him by being a superman, jumping off the top of the temple without being hurt. Satan even quoted from the Bible where it says God's angels will protect you and keep you safe. Jesus said, 'Yes, it does say that, and it also says, "Don't you dare tempt the Lord your God".' Jesus knew that this wasn't the way to get people to follow God. He had to do it by loving them, even if that took longer and meant he would get hurt.

Praying

Jesus, you know what it is like
to be tempted.
And you never gave in.
Please give me the strength
to stand up for what is right. Amen.

Activities

The worksheet has puzzle activities to reinforce the teaching, and instructions for planting seeds to grow during Lent.

Notes

GREEN FINGERS
You will need:
a flower pot
packet of seeds
FLOWER SEEDS
earth
water
Fill the pot with earth.
Sprinkle on the seeds.
Cover with a little earth.
Water well.
Wait, and keep watered.
This week's prayer
Jesus, you know what it is like to be tempted.
And you never gave in,
Please give me the strength to stand up for what is right.
Amen.
Temptation
If you do it I'll think you're brave
No one will notice
You want to, so it must be O.K.
If you don't like her why not be nasty to her?
If you tell the truth you'll get told off.
Are you scared then?
EAT ME
WHAT DID JESUS DO?
hard
it
would
get
chose
he
way
even
and
hurt
loving
He
the
was
though
HOW CAN WE DEAL WITH TEMPTATION?
Hold on to what you know is right
Remember how much God loves you
Be brave
Now do something you know will make God happy! (and enjoy it)

Second Sunday of Lent

Thought for the day

If only we will agree to put our faith in God, he will fill our lives with meaning and bring us safely to heaven.

Readings

Genesis 15:1-12, 17-18
Psalm 27
Philippians 3:17-4:1
Luke 13:31-35

Aim

To become familiar with the story of God's promise to Abraham.

Starter

A star count. Stick stars of all kinds all over the area, some hidden, some on view, and send the children round to count the stars. Reward the three closest answers.

Teaching

Have one leader to be Abraham and another to be the voice of God. Abraham starts by pacing up and down looking glum, and mumbling to himself.

God's voice What's up, Abraham? What's the trouble?

Abraham Oh Lord, sorry to moan, but I'm feeling a bit fed up.

God's voice Why, Abraham?

Abraham Well, you know I've got all these sheep and goats and everything, but I'm getting old. And I haven't got any children to leave it all to, and that makes me sad. It'll all go to someone else instead.

God's voice Abraham?

Abraham Yes, Lord?

God's voice Get up and go outside.

Abraham Get up and go outside? Oh, yes, all right Lord! Anything you say.

(He walks out, breathes deeply and looks up at the sky.)

Mmm! That's better. It's so beautiful outside. And those stars! *(Starts to count)* 1 . . . 2 . . . 24 . . . 309 . . . 4,082 . . . There's far too many to count. It's wonderful, Lord God. You are wonderful. You made all this. Blessed be your name for ever!

God's voice Thank you, Abraham! . . . Abraham?

Abraham Yes, Lord?

God's voice How many stars are there?

Abraham No idea, Lord. I was just trying to count them but I gave it up. Loads and loads.

God's voice Listen, Abraham. You won't be leaving all your belongings to someone else. You'll have a son to leave them to.

Abraham A son? Really?

God's voice Not only that, but I will make all your offspring to be as many as the stars in the sky. You will be the father of a great nation, Abraham!

Abraham As many as the stars in the sky! . . . A great nation! . . . My own son! Lord, you are amazing!

Praying

Dear Lord,
Abraham believed your promise.
He knew you would keep your word.
Help me to believe and trust you,
and help me to be the kind of person
other people can trust. Amen.

Activities

The worksheet has a Bible puzzle using stars which reinforces the teaching about God's promise and Abraham's faith. There are also instructions for making a moving model of the sky at night.

Notes

God keeps his promises

What did God tell Abraham to do?

Why was Abraham a bit sad?

What did God promise to Abraham?

Did Abraham believe God?

Genesis 15:1-12, 17-18

Colour this and cut out

Cover this with black or dark blue paper and draw or stick on lots of stars

This week's prayer

Dear Lord,
Abraham believed your promise.
He knew you would keep your word. Help me to believe and trust you.
And help me to be the kind of person other people cantrust.
Amen.

You will need:

scissors
black/blue paper
pencils
glue
sticky stars
split pin

What to do:

Fix Abraham in front of the sky with a split pin.
Use the tab to watch the sky move round during the night as Abraham counts the stars.

THIRD SUNDAY OF LENT

Thought for the day

We have God's invitation to come and drink freely of his Spirit, but if we keep refusing his offer it can eventually be withdrawn.

Readings

Isaiah 55:1-9
Psalm 63:1-8
1 Corinthians 10:1-13
Luke 13:1-9

Aim

To explore what we mean by 'thirsting for God'.

Starter

'What I really need is . . .' Split the children into groups and ask for things you really need which one person from each group brings to you. The first group to bring the correct object wins a point. Here are some ideas of what you didn't realise you needed so much: a left shoe, a coat with blue in it, glasses on a nose, a clean tissue/hanky, a pierced ear, a surprise, a song, four legs.

Teaching

Have a jug and pour out a glass of water. Talk about when we really want to drink a glass of water. The children will be describing (and therefore imagining) times they have been really thirsty. Show them some pictures of the land around Jerusalem so that they can imagine what it would be like living there. The people would know all about thirst and how it feels, and how our bodies long for water when thirsts threatens our survival.

Listen to the prophet's words in Isaiah, inviting people to drink. What does this kind of thirst feel like?

When your body is thirsty, you need to drink water. When your spirit is thirsty for goodness, right and truth in life, you need to drink in God's Spirit.

How do you know when you're thirsty for God?

Draw on a large glass: 'I need you in my life, Lord God'. When we come to God and say, 'I need you in my life, Lord God', we are telling God we are thirsty for him, because we know we need him. Whenever we know we want the best and right thing to happen and not just what would please us, we are thirsty for God. Whenever we notice something that isn't right and fair, and want to put it right, we are thirsty for God.

Whenever we see news on television that makes us sad, and we start wishing that people were not so cruel and greedy, and that people didn't have to die from dirty water or starvation, we are thirsty for God.

Whenever we want to be more loving, more honest, more trustworthy, or braver at standing up for what's right, then we're thirsty for God.

And being thirsty for God is one of the most important jobs we can do in life. And you probably often do it already. You don't have to be grown up to do it.

So . . . how do we drink?

Draw a well.

You pray. Get in touch with the 'water' supply which in this case is God. Tell him about your thirst; cry to him for the people you feel sorry for. Explain how you are feeling and what you long for. And remember that the God you are talking to is real, alive, and able to quench your thirst.

Praying

Waiting for your Spirit.

kneel with hands palms up, heads bowed; raise head and look up

Thirsty for your Spirit.

cup hands and bring to mouth to 'drink'

Touching us, Lord, as we pray;

touch fingertips together

filling our lives with you again,

stretch out arms with palms up

fall on us, Lord, as we call on you.

slowly raise arms upwards

From the song by Mick Gisbey

This can be said slowly to a quiet music background, sung along with the recorded music on tape or used with the music on page 128.

Activities

Use the directions on the worksheet to turn a drinking cup into a prayer. There is a puzzle to solve which helps the children look at the effects of God's Spirit in our lives, and prepares them for God's often surprising way of getting things done.

Notes

Thirsty for God

How to turn a drinking cup into a prayer. You will need:

2 clear plastic cups that fit inside each other

felt-tip pens

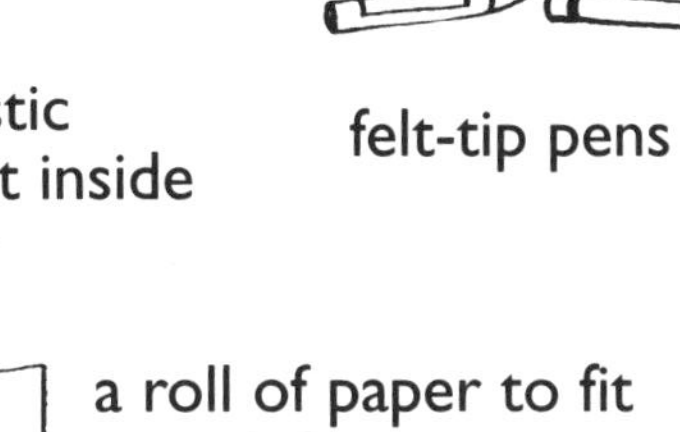

a roll of paper to fit round the cup

What you do:

1 On one side of the paper draw and colour the things in the world where you are thirsty for God to be and to use.

2 On the other side of the paper draw and colour the words THANK YOU, MY GOD!

3 Fix the paper round the cup and fix the second cup around that.

4 As you feel thirsty and look at the drink, pray for what you drew. As you enjoy drinking, thank God for hearing your prayer.

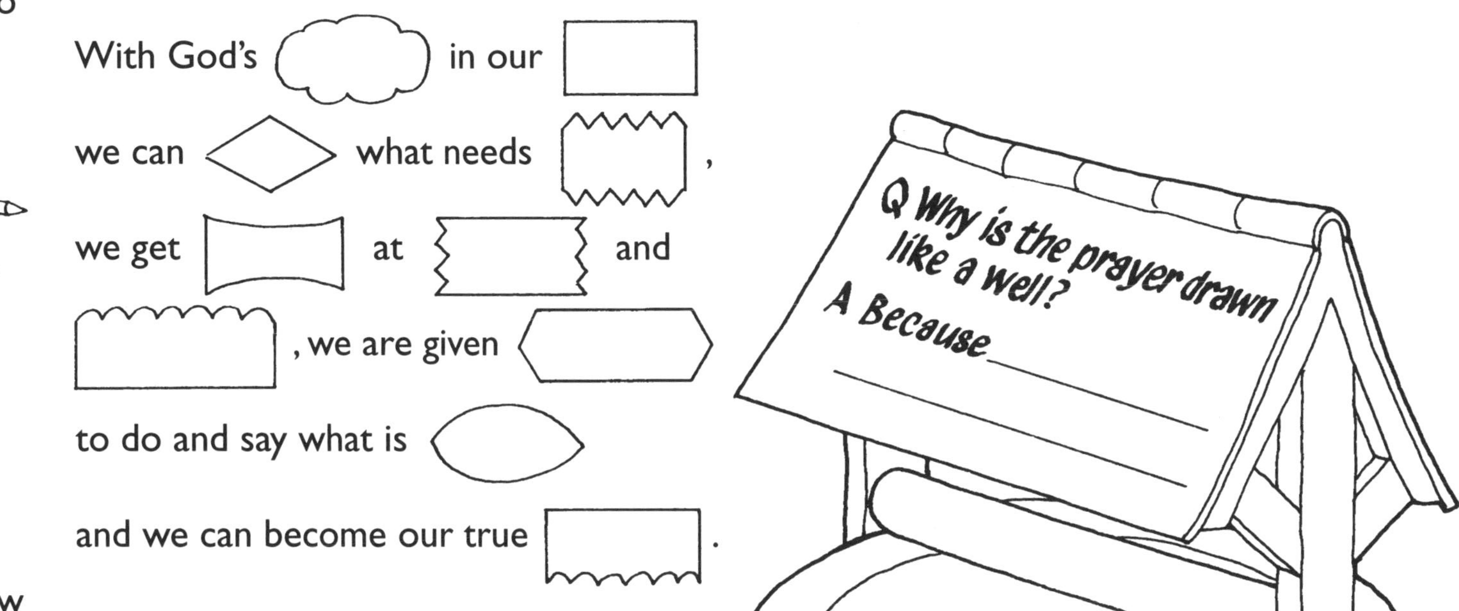

Put some quiet music on while you pray, and take your time. You can do the actions, too.

FOURTH SUNDAY OF LENT: MOTHERING SUNDAY

Thought for the day

While we are here in this life, given one another to care for, we can learn the lessons of mutual love and support and shared suffering.

Readings

Exodus 2:1-10 or 1 Samuel 1:20-28
Psalm 34:11-20 or Psalm 127:1-4
2 Corinthians 1:3-7 or Colossians 3:12-17
Luke 2:33-35 or John 19:25-27

Activities

Today is not one for learning separately but for celebrating and learning together. Use some of the all-age suggestions from the *Living Stones* Complete Resource Book and involve the children and young people in the music group or choir, as servers, welcomers, collectors of the offering, and so on. Provide shakers and bells for the younger ones to play during one or two hymns, and streamers to wave. Gather the children round the altar for the eucharistic prayer and choose hymns where the meaning is accessible to everyone.

Have materials for making cards available.

Notes

How to make chocolate surprises
You will need
Dates
Cherries
Raisins
and
melted chocolate–take care
What you do
1. Dip the fruits in the melted chocolate and leave to set on foil.
2. Pack into the box and give to your Mum.
Cover an empty box with wrapping paper
Cut up some coloured paper in strips and put in the box
How to give your mum a tasty surprise!
Make a card to go with your surprise. On the front you can draw and colour your Mum!
Thanks!
Mum

FIFTH SUNDAY OF LENT

Thought for the day

When we are privileged to share in Christ's suffering, we also share in his new life.

Readings

Isaiah 43:16-21
Psalm 126
Philippians 3:4b-14
John 12:1-8

Aim

To become familiar with John's version of the story of Jesus' anointing.

Starter

Have a number of smells for the children to try and identify. Such things as an onion, grated chocolate, a cloth dipped in bleach, chopped grass, mustard, vinegar, and prawn cocktail flavoured crisps are placed in plastic boxes with foil on the top. Poke holes in the foil just before use.

Teaching

Spread a cloth down in the centre of the group and lay it with bowls of raisins, grapes and crisps. Have two leaders telling the story between them, as if they are Mary and Martha or Lazarus talking over what happened at the meal. They hand round the food to people as they talk about laying on this celebration meal for Jesus and his friends. They remember how Jesus had brought their brother back to life, and how his friendship has made their lives so happy. Mary explains how Martha showed her love for their friend by serving a wonderful meal, something she's really good at, and Martha explains what Mary did while Mary acts it out. Discreetly spray some perfume into the air at this point so that the fragrance is all around. Mention Judas objecting to the waste of money, and have one of the sisters hinting at his real reason for objecting. Then the sisters recall what Jesus said – the way he told them to leave Mary alone and stop nagging, because what she had done was very beautiful. She was preparing his body for burial. Mary and Martha can express their sadness as they remember all Jesus' suffering, but they end by reminding each other that even that terrible suffering was made beautiful by the love it showed us all.

Praying

No wonder people loved you, Jesus.
I'd love to have met you
and talked to you face to face,
and invited you to our house for tea.
I may not be able to see you now,
but I know you're just as much alive
as you were then.
Still loving us, still forgiving us,
still wanting us as your friends.
Thank you, Jesus,
for being the best friend ever! Amen.

Activities

On the worksheet there is a wordsearch which consolidates their understanding of today's Gospel, and instructions for making their own potpourri and container to give to someone they love and want to thank. The ingredients are not expensive, but will need some preparation before the session. If your church ever uses incense (and there is no reason why the sense of smell should just be confined to one tradition!) older children will enjoy being shown the mechanics of it, and seeing it as another expression of our offering of thanks and praise to God.

Notes

How to make your own Pot-pourri

To keep or give away to a friend

You need
- Orange peel
- lemon peel
- cloves
- few drops of perfumed oil
- daisies
- dried grass
- Primrose heads

Cut the peel in strips with scissors.
Dry the primroses, daisies and grass in a paper bag for a few days.
Dry the peel in an oven on a low heat.
Mix all the ingredients together.
Stir in the perfumed oil.
Put in a pot to smell beautiful.

This week's prayer

No wonder people loved you, Jesus. I'd love to have met you and talked to you face to face, and invited you to our house for tea.
I may not be able to see you now, but I know you're just as much alive as you were then. Still loving us, still forgiving us, still wanting us as your friends.
Thank you, Jesus, for being THE BEST FRIEND EVER!
Amen.

One day JESUS was invited to a special MEAL with his friends, MARY, MARTHA and LAZARUS. They all enjoyed the FOOD. Then Mary got some PERFUME and started to ANOINT Jesus' FEET. Judas said it was a WASTE of MONEY. Jesus told them to stop getting at Mary, because what she had done was to show her LOVE and that was BEAUTIFUL.

M	A	R	Y	X	E	Z	S	Y	B
E	W	U	P	E	R	F	U	M	E
A	L	A	Z	A	R	U	S	L	A
L	T	F	E	E	T	F	E	O	U
A	L	J	C	V	N	D	J	V	T
W	A	S	T	E	I	Q	G	E	I
S	K	B	I	M	O	N	E	Y	F
F	O	O	D	A	N	H	O	N	U
M	A	R	T	H	A	M	P	R	L

Palm Sunday

Thought for the day

As Jesus rides into Jerusalem on a donkey, and the crowds welcome him, we sense both the joy at the Messiah being acclaimed, and the heaviness of his suffering which follows. Jesus' mission is drawing to its fulfilment.

Readings

Liturgy of the Palms:
Luke 19:28-40
Psalm 118:1-2, 19-29

Liturgy of the Passion:
Isaiah 50:4-9a
Psalm 31:9-16
Philippians 2:5-11
Luke 22:14-23:56 or Luke 23:1-49

Aim

To get to know the events of Palm Sunday and think about its significance.

Starter

Stop, go, cheer! Make a red 'Stop' and a green 'Go' sign, and a crown. Have the words for shouting written up large and with a festive feel. When the red sign is shown they have to freeze; when the green sign is shown they can move around the room; and when the crown is shown they shout 'Blessed is he who comes in the name of the Lord! Hosanna in the highest!' Sometimes the green sign and the crown can be shown together.

Teaching

The children's classic book *Donkey's glory* (Nan Goodall) includes the story from the donkey's point of view, and the Palm Tree series includes *Jesus on a donkey* which tells the story from the point of view of one of the children. Pictures to accompany the telling can be copied on to acetates and shown on an OHP, or simply held up and shared.

Praying

Holy, holy, holy, Lord,
God of power and might!
Heaven and earth are full of your glory;
Hosanna in the highest!
Blessed is he who comes in the name of the Lord.
Hosanna in the highest!

Activities

On the worksheet there are instructions for making a picture in relief using aluminium foil and the template provided. The children may also be joining in with the parish procession, waving streamers, singing and dancing. Another activity on the sheet involves decoding a message which can be checked by reading Luke's account of the entry into Jerusalem.

Notes

Palm Sunday

How to make a picture in relief.

You will need:

cooking foil

newspaper

a clip

blunt pencil and a biro

What you do.

Lay the shiny side of the foil on newspaper and the guide picture on top. Draw over the lines and experiment with shading. Keep the papers still.

Some of the Pharisees said to Jesus, 'Teacher, tell your followers not to say these things!'

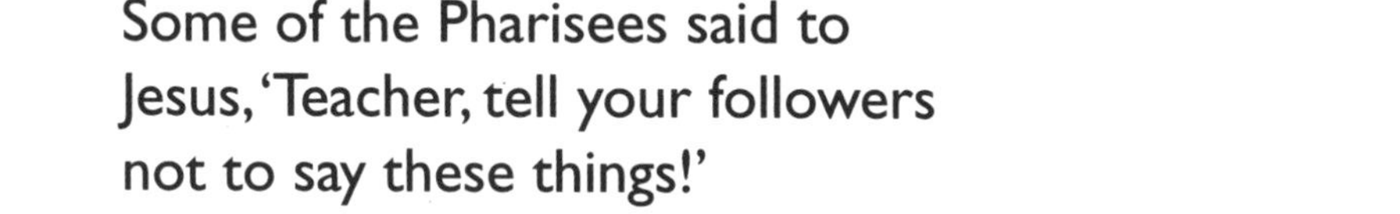

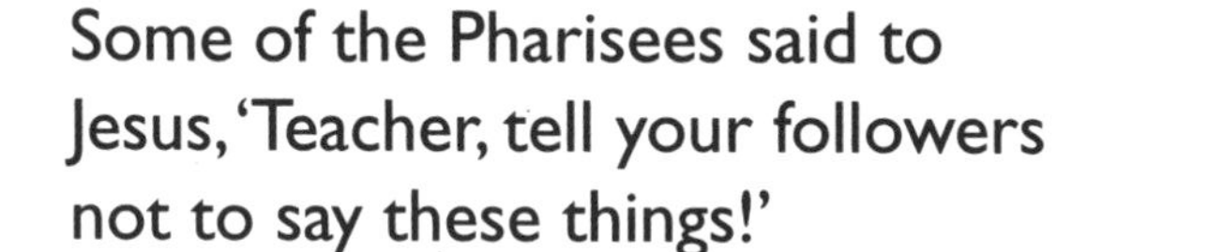

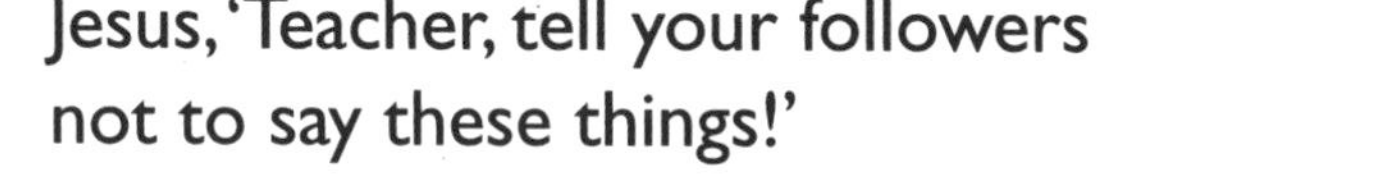

But Jesus answered,

'It ellyo u,i fmyfo llo wersd on'ts ayt heset hings,t hent hest onesw illc ryout.'

Code breaker
1, 4, 3, 2,
2, 9, 4, 3,
5, 6, 4, 3,
6, 4, 3, 3.

Number of letters in each word

Holy, holy, holy, Lord.
God of power and might!
Heaven and earth are full of your glory,
HOSANNA IN THE HIGHEST!
Blessed is he who comes in the name of the Lord.
Hosanna in the highest.

EASTER

Easter Day

If possible, it is recommended that the children and young people are in church with the other age groups today. Use and adapt some of the all-age ideas from the *Living Stones* Complete Resource Book, and involve the children and young people in some of the music and in the decorating of the church.

Thought for the day

It is true. Jesus is alive for all time. The Lord of life cannot be held by death. God's victory over sin and death means that new life for us is a reality.

Readings

Acts 10:34-43 or Isaiah 65:17-25
Psalm 118:1-2, 14-24
1 Corinthians 15:19-26 or Acts 10:34-43
John 20:1-18 or Luke 24:1-12

Aim

To teach them about the first Easter.

Starter

Have an Easter egg hunt, preferably outside if this is safe and practical.

Teaching

Have two leaders as the women, talking over what happened that morning. It needs to be in a chatty, informal style, rather as two friends might talk over their experience of bumping into someone really famous who helped them pick up the shopping they had dropped. Only this experience of meeting the risen Jesus is so extraordinary that both of them are still fairly dazed by it.

Praying

Christ has died.
Christ is risen.
Christ will come again.
Alleluia!

Activities

On the worksheet there are instructions for making a cross of flowers. Each child will need a piece of oasis and access to either a garden or a selection of small flowers. There is also a picture of the first Easter morning to complete and colour.

Notes

You will need:

a cross cut out of oasis

water

some small flowers

3 cocktail sticks

paper, pens and scissors

This week's prayer. Say it as you look at your cross.

Christ has died.
Christ is risen.
Christ will come again.
Alleluia!

HOW TO MAKE A CROSS WHICH SAYS 'JESUS IS ALIVE!'

What to do:

1 Write the words Jesus is alive on paper.

2 Poke on to the sticks like this.

3 Soak the oasis well.

4 Arrange the flowers and leaves.

5 Fix the sticks in between the flowers.

6 Keep the cross wet.

Can you help the artist finish this picture? Read Luke 24:1-12 to help you.

Second Sunday of Easter

Thought for the day

Having seen Jesus in person, the disciples are convinced of the Resurrection. We too can meet him personally.

Readings

Acts 5:27-32
Psalm 118:14-29 or Psalm 150
Revelation 1:4-8
John 20:19-31

Aim

To help them see the value of the apostles' eyewitness accounts.

Starter

Wink murder. All stand in a circle. One person is the detective, and goes outside while the murderer is chosen. When the detective returns she has to try and work out who the murderer is. The murderer kills people by winking at them, and they die in bloodcurdling fashion.

Teaching

Have one of the leaders and a few children brought in chains to the rest of the children, who are sitting formally in chairs as the Sanhedrin. Another leader is the High Priest, and talks to the children about the way these people have been breaking their law by telling everyone that Jesus is not dead but alive. Peter is interviewed on trial, and tells all the children why they know for certain that Jesus is alive. They have actually seen him! Break into the scene and ask Peter and Thomas if they would mind coming along to meet the children, as they'd like to know more about it. Peter and Thomas agree, and the children can be moved into a less formal group. The apostles are pleased to see them (they think they might have seen them somewhere before!) and you can then ask Peter to tell you all about Easter Sunday evening, and Thomas about what happened the following week. No wonder they are so certain that Jesus really is alive!

Praying

Jesus,
I have heard the witness
of those who saw you alive
after the Resurrection,
and I believe they told the truth.
You are alive,
and I can live my life
in your company!
Thank you, Jesus.

Activities

On the sheet there is an activity which involves the children being witnesses themselves. This will help them understand the importance of being a witness, and see how it feels to know something is true because you have seen it. They will need Bibles to look up the reference to Acts 5.

Notes

This is what you saw. Look at it for a minute, then cover it up.
Now you are called to be a witness

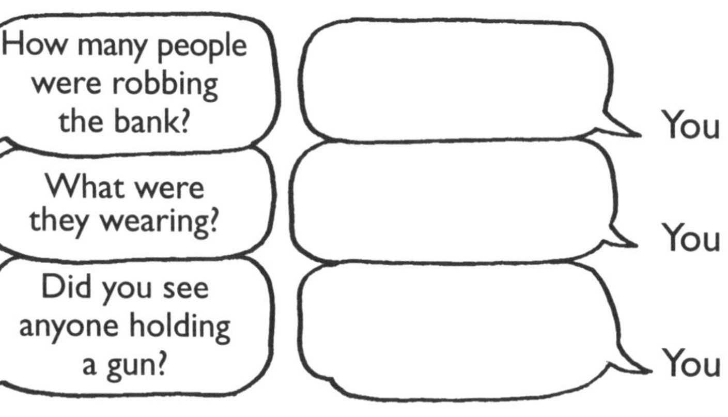

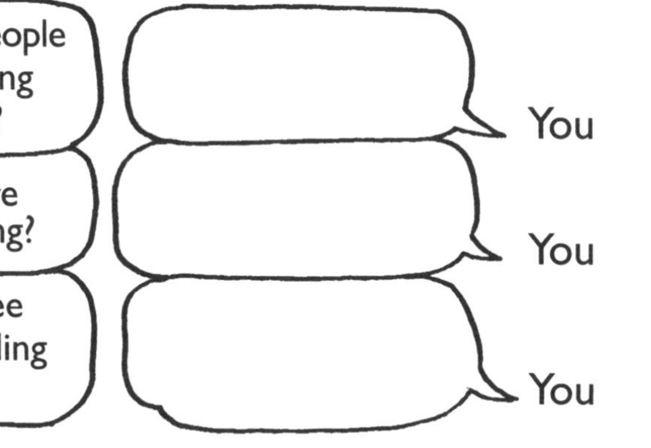

Witnesses are very important

Why is Peter so sure that Jesus, who was put to death, is alive again?
Acts 5 verse 32
'We ______________________,
______________________'

This week's prayer

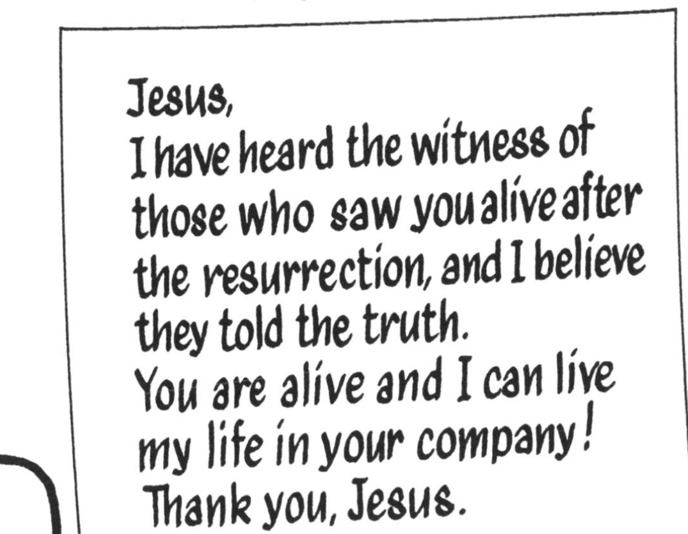
Jesus,
I have heard the witness of those who saw you alive after the resurrection, and I believe they told the truth.
You are alive and I can live my life in your company!
Thank you, Jesus.

O T M A S H

Who believed when he had seen Jesus?

THIRD SUNDAY OF EASTER

Thought for the day

Those who know Jesus and recognise that he is the anointed Saviour are commissioned to go out as his witnesses to proclaim the good news.

Readings

Acts 9:1-6 (7-20)
Psalm 30
Revelation 5:11-14
John 21:1-19

Aim

For them to connect Peter's previous denial with today's commitment and commissioning.

Starter

Sit in a circle and go on a campfire-style 'lion hunt'. The journey to the cave – through short grass, long grass, sticky mud, water and so on – is repeated at speed in the other direction on the return journey. Today we're going to look at the way we sometimes have to go back the way we came to put things right in our lives.

Teaching

Have a fishing net (such as a net curtain), some shiny paper fish, some driftwood and matches, and a mirror, explaining that all these come into today's story. Read the story from the *International Children's Version* or the *Good News Bible*, asking the children to listen out for when the objects are mentioned. This will help to focus their listening, and they will also notice that the matches are there as a sign of the driftwood being a fire, and there is no mention of a mirror. Explain that the mirror is, like the matches, a sign for something that is going on in the story.

Show people their faces in the mirror and point out that by doing this you are helping them to see for themselves what they look like. In our story Jesus is helping Peter to see what he is really like, and in our lives Jesus helps each of us to see what we are like as people. Some things we know already. You probably know if you are a kind person, or if you worry a lot, or if you get easily upset, or if everything makes you laugh. You might already know whether you are good or bad at telling the truth, making up quickly after an argument, or cheering up your friends. That's good. Jesus wants us to get to know ourselves.

Sometimes people get frightened by what they find out about themselves. Perhaps they would like to think they were kind, but they find out that really they are quite unkind. Peter wanted to be the kind of person who would stick up for Jesus however dangerous it became, but he found out on Good Friday that he was actually a bit of a coward. Three times he had denied he even knew Jesus.

Jesus wanted to show him that he still loved him, and it was OK to be like he really was, so long as he didn't pretend he was different. That way Jesus could help him learn to be the brave person he wanted to be. Three times Jesus gave Peter the chance to say he loved him, so that the past was put right.

And Jesus says to us, 'It's OK to be the person you are. You don't need to pretend you're different. Together we can work on the things you find hard.'

Praying

Jesus, you're right.
There isn't any point in pretending with you,
because you know me as I really am.
I'm glad I'm me, if you're glad I'm me!
Let's work together
on those things I find hard. Amen.

Activities

The separate figures on the sheet can be coloured and cut out and stuck on to a background of blue and yellow sugar paper. Other things can be added, such as pieces of net and shiny fish, to create a collage picture. There is also an activity on the sheet to link Peter's denial with this fresh chance to put things right.

Notes

This week's prayer

Jesus, you're right.
There isn't any point in pretending
with you, because you know me
as I really am.
I'm glad I'm me, if you're glad
I'm me!
Let's work together on those things
I find hard.
Amen.

Colour and cut out these pictures and mount them on a background of sky, sand and sea. Add woolly clouds, shiny fish and a sun.

FOURTH SUNDAY OF EASTER

Thought for the day

Asked if he really is the Christ, Jesus directs his questioners to look at his life in action and see for themselves that he and the Father are one.

Readings

Acts 9:36-43
Psalm 23
Revelation 7:9-17
John 10:22-30

Aim

To understand that we can look at the signs to draw conclusions about who Jesus is.

Starter

Detectives. Take the group around outside the church to look for clues from which they can work out what has been going on and who has been there recently. They might notice things like cigarette ends, footprints in the mud, evidence of rain or frost, left-over confetti from a wedding, or bird feathers and dying blossom on the ground. From the evidence they can build up a picture of events, even though they haven't actually witnessed them.

Teaching

Read today's Gospel with the children acting it out. Have the words spoken in verse 24 written up, so that all the children, gathering round Jesus, can ask the question. Then go over the reading in a short quiz: What time of year was it? Where was Jesus for Hanukkah? What did the Jewish people ask him? What did Jesus tell them to look at to find the answer to their question?

Remind the children of what they have managed to find out today by looking at the signs around the church. Using a large sheet of paper to record ideas, have them working in small groups to draw or write on their paper any miracles they can remember Jesus doing. Then have each group feeding back to the main group. Display all the ideas and prompt where necessary. This will be useful both for the children to recall the works of Jesus, and for you to notice any gaps in their experience – and to encourage you by finding out how much they actually remember!

Praying

Jesus, we have looked at the clues
and we can see
that you must really be
the Christ, the Son of God.
Help those who doubt you
to realise the truth. Amen.

Activities

The worksheet picks up on the search for signs in a picture of a windy day. There are visual clues to help them recall some of the miracles and signs narrated in the Gospels, so that they can do what the coded message suggests. Sing *Jesus is greater than the greatest heroes* (No. 122, *The Children's Hymn Book*, Kevin Mayhew Ltd, 1997).

Notes

How can you tell the wind is blowing?

When the people asked Jesus if he was really the Christ, he said:

What signs do these help you remember?

A	C	D	E	F	H	I	K

L	M	N	O	P	R	S	T	Y

This week's prayer

Jesus, we have looked at the clues and we can see that you must really be the Christ, the Son of God. Help those who doubt you to realise the truth.

Amen.

FIFTH SUNDAY OF EASTER

Thought for the day

Christ, breaking through the barrier of sin and death, allows us to break into an entirely new way of living which continues into eternity.

Readings

Acts 11:1-18
Psalm 148
Revelation 21:1-6
John 13:31-35

Aim

To explore the nature of friendship and what it means to be God's friend.

Starter

If you can borrow a parachute, some parachute games would be excellent, as they help develop the qualities of sharing and co-operation. Alternatively play some circle games, such as passing the smile or passing the hand squeeze, and place-changing. (In this everyone makes a drum roll with hands on thighs, and chants, 'Is it you, is it me, who will it be? Who will it be?' Then the leader calls out the category, such as those who ate Cocopops for breakfast, those who are wearing stripes, or those who have a sister, and these people get up and change places.

Teaching

Explain that Jesus told his disciples they were to love one another. The way other people will recognise that we are Jesus' friends is by the way we love one another. If we don't live like that, it really means we are not his friends. Who do you think can be one of Jesus' friends? Is it only those brought up to go to church? Or only the ones who don't have bad tempers? Or only the ones who can read the Bible? (They can think about this; we'll talk about it after the story.)

Tell this story from the Early Church of how Peter had to learn something about who can be a friend of Jesus. After Peter has introduced himself, and one of the leaders has welcomed him and asked him to tell the children what happened, the story can be read directly from Acts 11, starting at verse 5, providing Peter is really familiar with it and can read it with feeling. Otherwise, he can memorise the gist of it and 'chat' his story. It is so important that any reading of Scripture lives for the children.

After the story, go back to the question you left the children to think about, and in a circle, so that all have a chance to speak, share their ideas.

Praying

Jesus, you are my friend
as well as my Lord and Saviour.
Please teach me to be a good friend
to others
all my life. Amen.

Activities

On the worksheet the children are encouraged to look at the qualities of a good friend, and I have included several things which may or may not be considered necessary, as well as some obvious choices. It is valuable for children of this age to start looking at the values they are living by, so that they learn to make thoughtful choices in the way they live.

Notes

What makes a good friend?

They share with you

They won't tell your secrets to anyone else

They make you feel happy

They don't let you down

They are less clever than you

They stick up for you

They support the same team

They help you

They listen to what you say

They tell you what to do and which music to like

They like the same music

They think you're nice

They like you unless other people are there

They buy you expensive presents

They don't boss you around

They are fun to be with

They tell you if you've upset them

Put a ring round the things that make a good friend

Jesus said, 'You are my friends, if . . .

John 13.33

How to show people what a good friend Jesus is.

Draw and colour your ideas on circles of paper.

Stick the ideas on a cross shape made of wallpaper.

Show the cross in the hall or at your school or in the library.

This week's prayer

Jesus, you are my friend
as well as my Lord and Saviour.
Please teach me to be a good
friend to others
all my life.
Amen.

Sixth Sunday of Easter

Thought for the day

The continuing presence of God, as Holy Spirit, leads us, as Jesus promised, into a personally guided outreach to all nations.

Readings

Acts 16:9-15
Psalm 67
Revelation 21:10, 22-22:5
John 14:23-29 or John 5:1-9

Aim

To look at God's provision for us in the leading and guidance of the Holy Spirit.

Starter

Pair the children up and blindfold one of the pair. They take it in turns to lead the blindfolded one around the grounds, taking great care to protect each other from danger.

Teaching

Talk over how it felt to be unable to see, and how it helped to have a friend to help us travel safely. When Jesus was with his friends at the last supper he talked to them about having to leave them. They were very sad and rather anxious at the thought of living without their good and wise friend there in person. Jesus had always been able to sort out their fears, cheer them up, get them to make up after arguments, and point out the right things to do. How on earth would they be able to cope without him? And how would they be brave enough to tell other people about him when they knew that would put them in danger?

Read the Gospel for today, asking them to listen out for a promise Jesus gave. They can put their hands up when they hear it, and John 14:23 can be displayed for everyone to read together. So the disciples (and that includes us) were not going to be left like orphans to manage on their own. Somehow God would be with them, in a real and personal way, even though it wouldn't be a person they could see physically.

To get just one idea of how this worked out, tell the children about a time after the Resurrection, when Paul and his friends were travelling round telling people about the God of love. Tell them how the Spirit stopped them going to some places they planned, and led them straight to another place, where some people were ready to hear the good news and become Christians. They can read about it in Acts 16. All over the world, and in each century, God the Holy Spirit is there, guiding people to understand God's will and open doors and nudge in the right direction.

Praying

You could sing *Waiting for your Spirit* (see pages 46 and 128) and have this prayer during the music interlude between verses:

Lord, I want to go wherever you need me.
Train me to notice
your quiet voice
showing me
the right way to live. Amen.

Activities

There is a short quiz and drawing activity on the worksheet to get the children thinking about the way loving involves taking thought and care for people. This may be an opportunity to recognise that rules their parents make may sometimes seem a pain but really they show that our parents care about us. There is also an opening to learn the need to listen to God's Spirit, and to practise this during the week. If there is time the children can colour some flags of different countries with the words 'God loves you' written in the appropriate language. These can be laid on the floor around the altar for people to see as they gather for communion.

Here are some languages to start you off:

French:	Dieu vous aime
German:	Gott liebt dich
Italian:	Dio ti ama
Spanish:	Dios te ama
Swahili:	Mungu anakupenda

Notes

What happens next?

Draw it here

When your parents say goodbye to you, do they

☐ leave you on your own for a week

☐ make sure there's someone to look after you

If your child minder is looking after you does he/she

☐ let you play ball on a busy road

☐ make sure you and your friends are safe

people us look us The
love ④ who after

Write it out in the right order.
The fourth word is done for you.

God's guiding Spirit is often very quiet – we need to listen carefully

Jesus says goodbye

(and gives a promise)
John 14 verse 23

Put these in order

ff VERY LOUD

pp very quiet

- bacon frying (c)
- a Boeing 747 taking off beside you (e)
- a piano being dropped downstairs (b)
- a pin dropping on a carpet (a)
- your mum singing in the bath (d)

To pray this week

Lord, I want to go wherever you need me. Train me to notice your quiet voice showing me the right way to live. Amen.

Ascension Day

Thought for the day

Having bought back our freedom with the giving of his life, Jesus enters into the full glory to which he is entitled.

Readings

Acts 1:1-11 or Daniel 7:9-14
Psalm 47 or Psalm 93
Ephesians 1:15-23 or Acts 1:1-11
Luke 24:44-53

Activities

It is likely that Ascension Day services for schools will not need a separate programme for children and young people. Children in church can work on this drawing and colouring activity during the sermon.

You may also like to consider using some of the all-age ideas given in the Complete Resource Book:

- Any artwork or writing that the children have done on what the Ascension is about can be displayed around the building, and time given in the service to looking at it.
- Have a beautiful helium balloon at the ready. Write on it an Ascension message that the children would like to send. After the service two representative children can let the balloon float away.
- Children can wave white and yellow streamers during some of the hymns.

Notes

Seventh Sunday of Easter

Thought for the day

Jesus lives for all time in glory; we can live the fullness of Resurrection life straight away.

Readings

Acts 16:16-34
Psalm 97
Revelation 22:12-14, 16-17, 20-21
John 17:20-26

Aim

To see the new life in action through the story of Paul and Silas.

Starter

Sitting in a circle, pass round a trophy type of cup. As each person holds it they name something they are able to do. Everyone responds, 'Thank you, God, for making us!'

Teaching

If the children have not been involved in the Ascension Day service, tell them about this last time the disciples met with Jesus, what he said to them, and where he was going. On a calendar they can work out how long Jesus had been around in his risen state since the Resurrection.

Today we are going to see an example of the kind of life Jesus' followers were living after Jesus had returned to heaven, and the Holy Spirit had been sent to equip the disciples for God's work.

Using puppets, have the story told stage by stage by the different characters involved. Start with the slave girl. Then Paul can take up the story of how the girl was healed. Then the owner tells how angry that made him. Silas can tell how he and Paul were arrested and beaten and thrown into prison. Another prisoner tells what he heard Paul and Silas doing at midnight, and how it cheered him up a bit, and Paul can shout above some earthquake noises to talk about the doors opening and so on. Now the jailer explains who he is and why he panicked, and how impressed he was by these two prisoners and their faith. Between them he and Paul can finish the story.

The puppets need only be very simple, made from wooden spoons with card faces, based on the pictures below.

Prisoner *Jailer*

Praying

Thank you, Jesus,
for the new life
you have won for me.
Fill me up
with the Spirit of God
so that I can live life
to the full. Amen.

Activities

This is such a good story that the children may like to turn it into a play, with sound effects. The worksheet reinforces the teaching with puzzles, and the children will need access to Bibles to solve them. There is also a question about the quality and direction of their own lives to think over, either in small groups or on their own during the week.

Look up John 17:20

Q. Who was Jesus praying for?

A. He was praying for

EHT SISCDILPE

and for

Acts 16:16-34

Our God reigns!

GOD

PRISON

PRAISES

PAUL

SILAS

STOCKS

BEATEN

Cut these shapes out carefully and arrange them on the black patch to make the answer to the question.

____ and _____ were in ______. They had been ______ and their feet put in the ______. Yet there they were, singing _______ to ___!

What is most important to me in life?

____

____

To pray this week

Thank you, Jesus
for the new life you have
won for me.
Fill me up with the Spirit
of God so I can live life
to the full.

Amen.

Pentecost

Thought for the day

As Jesus promised, the Holy Spirit is poured out on the apostles and the Church is born.

Readings

Acts 2:1-21 or Genesis 11:1-9
Psalm 104:24-34, 35b
Romans 8:14-17 or Acts 2:1-21
John 14:8-17 (25-27)

Aim

To become familiar with the events at Pentecost.

Starter

Play a game where the children are waiting expectantly but can only act when they hear the instruction. Here is one example. Everyone finds a space to stand in and the leader calls 'One . . . two . . . three . . . hop to the window/crawl like snakes/ pirouette round the table/score the winning goal.' (Choose a variety of activities to suit your group.)

Teaching

Remind the children of how, at the Ascension, the disciples had been told by Jesus to wait in Jerusalem for the gift of the Holy Spirit to come. They went back and spent time praying together so they would be ready for the Spirit when it came.

Have some of the children to be the apostles, waiting and praying together. As you read or tell them about the way the Spirit came, the other children can make the sound of an orchestrated rushing wind, and some can be given red crêpe-paper streamers to whirl around the place where the apostles are sitting. As the wind dies away and the disciples are left alone, tell the children how the Spirit had made them full of excitement and joy. They were longing to tell everyone about Jesus, and the way God loves us.

The apostles can now come running and dancing out to the crowd in the street, telling them that Jesus of Nazareth, who had been crucified, was the promised Messiah, the Christ, the Son of God. End with the people asking to be baptised and become his followers.

Praying

Fill my life,
Holy Spirit of God,
with joy and love and hope.
Live in me so I can show others
how much you love them. Amen.

Activities

Using the template on the worksheet the children can cut out lots of flames in red, yellow and orange. These can be given out to the rest of the congregation after the service. There is also a Pentecost wordsearch to reinforce the teaching. Finding words from 'Pentecost' will also help to familiarise them with this word.

Notes

Cut out flame shapes from red, yellow and orange paper. Cut out the messages. Stick them on the flames. Give them to people and pray for those you give them to.

H	O	L	Y	S	P	I	R	I	T
A	P	P	E	C	F	W	R	A	X
J	U	E	H	S	L	B	F	P	N
F	I	A	N	G	A	D	O	O	M
Z	J	C	B	T	M	W	L	S	H
T	A	E	Z	Q	E	I	W	T	R
P	M	R	D	R	D	C	J	L	Y
G	S	N	P	L	O	K	O	E	N
O	I	V	E	T	C	V	Y	S	K
W	Y	U	X	L	O	V	E	Q	T

PENTECOST
HOLY SPIRIT
LOVE JOY
WIND
APOSTLES
POWER
PEACE
FLAME

God loves you

Jesus is still alive

Seek and you will find

Come, Holy Spirit!

The Spirit gives life

The Spirit brings freedom

God's Spirit be with you

May God's love surround you

Ask and you will receive

Love, Joy, Peace

Let the Spirit of God enfold you

Holy Spirit, flood into my whole life!

Fill my life, Holy Spirit of God, with joy and love and hope. *Live in me* so I can show others how much you love them.

Amen.

ORDINARY TIME

TRINITY SUNDAY

Thought for the day

The unique nature of God is celebrated today, as we reflect on the truth that God is Creator, Redeemer and Life-giver.

Readings

Proverbs 8:1-4, 22-31
Psalm 8
Romans 5:1-5
John 16:12-15

Aim

To understand more about the nature of God.

Starter

Set out different colours of paints and help them to do colour sums, like this:

Red + Yellow =
Yellow + Blue =
Red + Green =

Teaching

Beforehand prepare the word 'Trinity' on two pieces of card, with 'Tri' on one piece and 'Unity' on the other.

First look together at the colour sums, and point out the way that although we put clear yellow and clear blue in, you can't see them any more once they've turned green. They have become something different.

Today is called Trinity Sunday, and we're going to look at what that means. Show the cards as 'Trinity'. Then put the 'Unity' bit down and concentrate on the 'Tri'. Talk about words they know which have this in them, such as tricycle, tripod and triangle. Between you work out from these words what 'Tri' means. What has three got to do with God? Draw three dots on a sheet of paper and name them with their help, God the Father, God the Son and God the Holy Spirit.

Now pick up the 'Unity' section. Block off the 'y' and ask what words they know with 'unit' in them, such as united, unit, and unite. If anyone can count in French you can ask them what 'un' means in French. Work out together the meaning of 'Unity'. What has this got to do with God? Draw lines joining the three dots together to form a triangle and explain that there is only one God. But unlike the colours we made, we can still see the three different 'colours' of God in his nature. That's why the Church has squashed the two words 'Tri' and 'Unity' together, to make a word that tries to understand God better. Fix the two pieces of card together again, and put the word next to the drawing.

Praying

Glory be to God the Father,
Glory be to God the Son,
Glory be to God the Spirit,
Holy Trinity, three in one!

Activities

There are instructions on the worksheet for making a Trinity bookmark using clover leaves and sticky-backed plastic. An alternative method is to use clover-leaf shapes cut from green paper. There are some other puzzles to solve, and a story of Patrick and the child on the beach.

Notes

Tell your family
what it means.

Saint Patrick was on the beach trying to understand the Trinity. He watched a child trying to fill a hole in the sand with sea water. Patrick went over to him. 'You'll never manage that, you know,' he said. 'The water will keep draining away.' The child replied, 'And neither will you ever manage to understand the Trinity.'

Q How can you get through an A4 sheet of paper?

A Cut it like this:

Here

and here

HOW TO MAKE A CLOVER BOOKMARK

You will need

a peg

coloured card and scissors

clover

sticky backed plastic

What you do

Cut this shape from card. Stick clover leaves on it. Cover with plastic. Stick to the peg.

To pray this week

Glory be to God the Father.
Glory be to God the Son.
Glory be to God the Spirit.
Holy Trinity, 3 in 1 !

PROPER 4

Sunday between 29 May and 4 June inclusive
(if after Trinity Sunday)

Thought for the day

The good news we have been given is not just for us, but to pass on to the rest of the world.

Readings

1 Kings 18:20-21 (22-29), 30-39
or 1 Kings 8:22-23, 41-43
Psalm 96 or Psalm 96:1-9
Galatians 1:1-12
Luke 7:1-10

Aim

To learn about the prophets' competition and the value of example in spreading the faith.

Starter

Have a beat-the-clock activity, where each person tries the same challenge and the one with the quickest time is the winner. Activities might be dressing up in thick gloves and eating a mini chocolate bar with a knife and fork, or transferring dried peas from one container to another using a straw.

Teaching

Tell the children that today we are going to hear about another competition – rather an unusual one. One of the children can be Elijah, who can be dressed in a tunic and rope belt. Others are the prophets of Baal. The rest of the children are the crowd who came out to watch. As you tell the story, the children act it out. Give someone a tin sheet to rattle when the lightning falls, and have someone primed to take a flash photo at the same time, so the sudden bright light surprises the actors as well as the people in Elijah's time. Everyone can shout the words 'The Lord is God! The Lord is God!' at the end.

Praying

Dear Jesus,
we pray for those
who have not heard of you
and do not know you.
Give us the opportunity
to share the good news
with someone today. Amen.

Activities

The worksheet encourages them to look at how they can spread the good news, and gives examples of people who have been called to tell others the Gospel even though it put them in danger.

Notes

Draw or write what you would want people to know about God.

To pray this week

Dear Jesus,
We pray for those who have not heard of you and do not know you. Give us the opportunity to share the good news with someone today.
Amen.

Father Damien

LEPROSY Island

Father Damien chose to live on an island where Lepers had to live, so that he could teach them about God's love, and help them. He did get leprosy himself through working with the disease.

Brother Andrew

SMUGGLER of Bibles

Brother Andrew found out that people in parts of Russia and China were not allowed to have Bibles for sale. So he smuggled Bibles across the borders and made sure people could read the good news. He was often in great danger.

Jackie Pullinger

DRUGS city

Jackie Pullinger lived and worked with the drug addicts in Hong Kong. She wanted them to know the power of Jesus in their lives. As they started to trust her, many came to know God, and it changed their lives.

Proper 5

Sunday between 5 and 11 June inclusive
(if after Trinity Sunday)

Thought for the day

Our God is full of compassion; he hears our crying and it is his nature to rescue us.

Readings

1 Kings 17:8-16 (17-24) or 1 Kings 17:17-24
Psalm 146 or Psalm 30
Galatians 1:11-24
Luke 7:11-17

Aim

To get to know the story of Elijah and the widow.

Starter

Make some bread with oil and flour. It doesn't need kneading, it is quite quick to mix and shape, and can either be cooked straight away or taken home to bake. The recipe is given on the worksheet.

Teaching

Talk about the ingredients we used in the basic bread-making. As the oil and flour are mentioned, stand a jar and jug in the centre. Today's story is about some rather unusual oil and flour.

Once again have someone to dress up as Elijah. This will help familiarise the children with the prophet. Starting from the weather conditions here at the moment, talk about the drought that God had told Elijah about, so he could warn the king. God then told Elijah to go out into the countryside and use a brook in a deep ravine there. When that dried up, God sent Elijah to another place called Zarephath.

Now tell them the story, with Elijah and the widow and her son acting it out. The little rhyme about the oil and the flour can be written out so that everyone can join in:

Jar of flour will not run out,
jug of oil will not run dry
until the day
God sends you rain again.

Praying

Using the oil and flour and their loaves as a focus, pray for those who are in a drought at the moment and whose harvests have failed. Pray for those who are so hungry that they are ill with hunger. Pray for those who have no food to give their children. Pray for those who have not yet learned how to share. Between each child leading the sections, everyone prays, 'Lord, have mercy!'

Activities

On a world map find out where Zarephath is. (It's midway between Tyre and Sidon, on the Mediterranean coast.) The worksheet encourages them to empathise with the widow, and there is also a quiz on the Luke reading. The children can either read the story first and then have a go at the quiz, or work on both together.

Notes

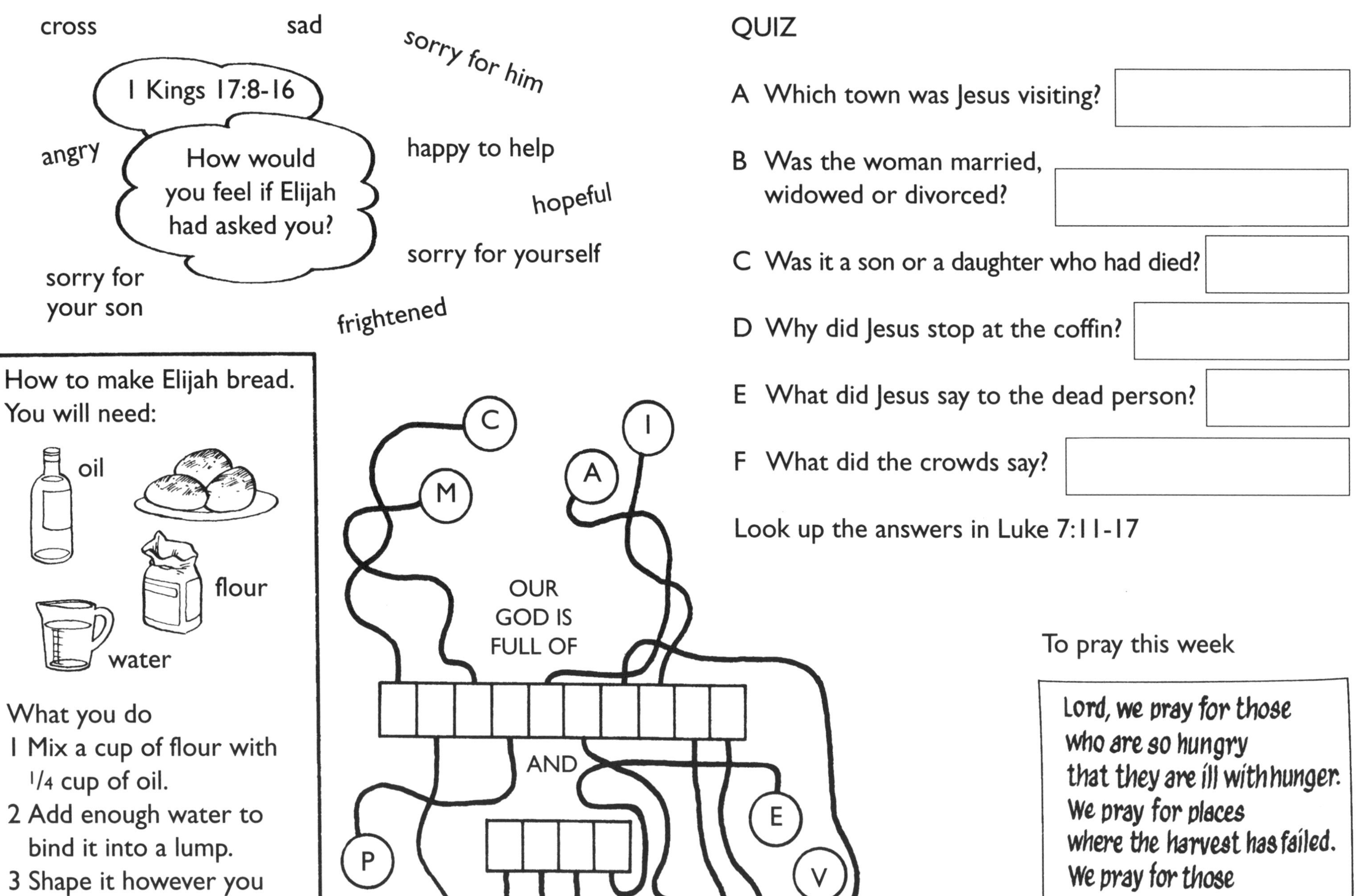

QUIZ

A Which town was Jesus visiting?

B Was the woman married, widowed or divorced?

C Was it a son or a daughter who had died?

D Why did Jesus stop at the coffin?

E What did Jesus say to the dead person?

F What did the crowds say?

Look up the answers in Luke 7:11-17

How to make Elijah bread.
You will need:

oil

flour

water

What you do

1 Mix a cup of flour with 1/4 cup of oil.

2 Add enough water to bind it into a lump.

3 Shape it however you want.

4 Bake for about 15 minutes in a hot oven.

To pray this week

Lord, we pray for those
who are so hungry
that they are ill with hunger.
We pray for places
where the harvest has failed.
We pray for those
who have no food
to give their children.
Lord, have mercy.

Proper 6

Sunday between 12 and 18 June inclusive
(if after Trinity Sunday)

Thought for the day

God has the authority and the desire to forgive our sins completely and set us free from guilt.

Readings

1 Kings 21:1-10 (11-14), 15-21a
or 2 Samuel 11:26-12:10, 13-15
Psalm 5:1-8 or Psalm 32
Galatians 2:15-21
Luke 7:36-8:3

Aim

To get to know the story of Naboth's vineyard and its implications for them.

Starter

Sit in a circle. Each person in turn says three things about someone in the circle (only positives allowed), and everyone guesses who it is. Each person can only be described once, which means that everyone gets a turn to be described. Or play 'Stuck in the mud', which is a kind of 'tag'. When caught, you stand with arms and legs apart, stuck in the mud, unless someone crawls between your legs to set you free again.

Teaching

Tell the story with different children acting it out as it is narrated. Jezebel's letter can be written out (simplifying it for your group) and Jezebel can read it out. Balls of white paper can be thrown as stones, and simple costumes worn (such as crowns and cloaks for the King and Queen, tea-towel head-dresses for Naboth and his accusers, and a piece of rough cloth for Elijah.

Praying

Talk about our need to recognise and admit to God the times when we let him down by our unloving, selfish behaviour, knowing that he is able to forgive us.

Lord God,
thank you for helping me do good today,
when I . . .
I am sorry that I let you down
and hurt others
when I . . .
Please forgive me
and help me put it right.
Thank you, Lord God,
for forgiving me!

Activities

On the worksheet there are instructions for making a 'soul mirror'; each child will need either a small hand mirror or shiny mirror paper. There is also an activity to reinforce the teaching and encourage discussion about the story.

Notes

Who did what?
This person thought it was fine to get people killed if they stood in your way. It's weak to be kind.
King Ahab
Naboth
This person got punished by death for a crime he hadn't committed. He was the victim of someone else's sin.
This person spoke God's anger at the cruel and unfair behaviour. God hates evil.
Queen Jezebel
This person sulked when he couldn't get his own way.
Elijah
How to make a mirror to check your behaviour in
You will need
a small mirror
bluetack
paper
scissors
What you do
1 Cut the paper to the size of the mirror
2 Draw a cross on it and cut it out
3 Write on the surrounding paper: 'Look at my love for you. How was your love today?'
Use your 'soul mirror' at night and let God forgive you.
To pray during the week
Lord God,
Thank you for helping me do good today when I..........
I am sorry that I let you down and hurt others when I..........
Please forgive me, and help me put it right.
Thank you, Lord God, for forgiving me!

Proper 7

Sunday between 19 and 25 June inclusive
(if after Trinity Sunday)

Thought for the day

God is close through all our troubles, and can bring us safely through them.

Readings

1 Kings 19:1-4 (5-7), 8-15a or Isaiah 65:1-9
Psalms 42, 43 or Psalm 22:19-28
Galatians 3:23-29
Luke 8:26-39

Aim

To see how God looked after Elijah and the wild man, and how he looks after us, too.

Starter

Beforehand set up a wool trail at the children's waist height, and send them off blindfolded to follow it. Make sure plenty of helpers are around as this will be quite scary for some children. Don't make anyone do it who is very timid, but encourage most to take part, walking beside them for support.

Teaching

Talk about the trail, and how useful the wool was in leading us round the right way, even though it was still a strange feeling to be stumbling along unable to see. Explain how for most people life can seem scary and bewildering sometimes, and God is always there, even though we can't see him, helping us along and pointing out the way.

Tell the Elijah story using the symbols from the all-stage talk in the *Living Stones* Complete Resource Book as follows:

- a small loaf of bread and a pillow – to show that God looks after us and starts by providing our practical needs;
- a calendar and a clock – to remind us that God gave Elijah time and didn't rush him during his troubles;
- writing paper and envelopes which help us to keep in touch with people going through sad times, just as God kept in contact with Elijah;
- a briefcase which is something people carry to work – God knew when Elijah was ready to move forward and he gave him a job to do. He will do the same with us.

Involve the children in providing the sound effects.

Praying

Whenever I am sad or lonely, Lord God,
I will remember that you know me
and you love me,
and I will put my trust in you,
and give you thanks and praise. Amen.

Activities

On the worksheet there are instructions for making a basket of love. These can be given out to people in the parish who are going through a sad or difficult time at the moment, with love from the children. The vicar, or priest in charge, can suggest people to receive the baskets.

Notes

How to make a basket of love

You will need

a small box

gift wrapping paper

glue

fresh or dried flowers

and oasis

a little gift (like sweets, a pot of jam, a flannel or a hanky)

A message

a small lid for the flowers

What you do

1 Cover the box with paper and decorate it how you like.
2 Arrange the flowers. (If you are using fresh flowers, wet the oasis first.)
3 Make and decorate the message.
4 Pack everything into the box.
5 Give it to someone who is going through a sad or painful time, to show them God's love.

To pray this week

Whenever I am sad or lonely,
Lord God, I will remember that
you know me and you love me,
and I will put my trust in you
and give you thanks and praise.
Amen.

C	F	G	S	X	B	D	E	S	E	R	T
H	D	E	A	E	Q	F	S	E	R	A	E
A	M	R	R	L	E	U	K	V	T	Z	L
I	G	A	P	A	I	I	M	A	Y	D	L
N	R	S	B	I	T	L	H	C	U	F	P
S	Q	E	B	R	G	D	E	M	O	N	S
P	Z	N	L	U	H	S	W	E	M	T	C
Q	V	E	O	B	J	L	E	G	I	O	N
Z	E	S	I	U	O	L	F	F	O	E	G

Luke 8:26-39
See if you can find these words
V. 26 G _ L _ _ _ _ _ and G _ R _ _ _ _ _ _ _
V. 27 D _ M _ _ _ _ , B _ R _ _ _ _ C _ V _ _
V. 29 C _ A _ _ _ _ , D _ S _ _ _
V. 30 L _ G _ _ _ V. 32 P _ G _
V. 39 T _ L _

PROPER 8

Sunday between 26 June and 2 July inclusive

Thought for the day

When we are called to follow Jesus, that means total commitment, with no half-measures.

Readings

2 Kings 2:1-2, 6-14 or 1 Kings 19:15-16, 19-21
Psalm 77:1-2, 11-20 or Psalm 16
Galatians 5:1, 13-25
Luke 9:51-62

Aim

To get to know the story of Elijah being taken up to heaven, and Elisha becoming his successor.

Starter

What's my line? In turn the children mime a job, and everyone has to guess what it is. The one who guesses correctly does the next mime, or you can work round the group circle.

Teaching

Prepare the different pictures for the story on card. Suggestions are given below.

Then tell the story using carpet tiles on the floor and move the pictures around as you talk. The cloak can be a piece of fabric placed on top of the Elijah picture, so that as he is taken off in the whirlwind, the cloak can fall and be picked up by Elisha. The river Jordan can be two blue silky scarves which are trailed over the landscape and can be pulled apart at the appropriate moment.

Praying

Lord God, here I am,
ready to do
whatever you need me to.
And, Lord, prepare me now
for what you would like me to do
in the future. Amen.

Activities

The worksheet explores the nature of vocation, with quotations from people in varied ministries. Talk through with the children the ministry they have in places no one but them can reach, such as in their families and friendships, in their playground and at their clubs. Jesus likes to use us where we are.

Notes

Being called by God to a particular job is sometimes known as having a

Here are some people talking about what they were called to do.

I felt God was calling me to serve him by teaching the children at church. They teach me as much as I teach them!

When I was 6 years old I knew I wanted to be a priest, and felt God had called me. I love helping people get to know God, though it can be hard work.

God gave us the idea of this rock band, and now we sing and play to young people and it's exciting to lead them to God through our music

I was already an athlete and when I became a Christian, God called me to use my work in sport to bring people to Christ. It makes life twice as exciting!

Draw in the rest of the landscape. (2 Kings 2:13-14)

2 Kings 2:14

now | Elijah? | the | is | Lord, | where | of | God | the

Knock knock.
Who's there?
Ivor.
Ivor who?
Ivor message for you, if only you'd listen!

Knock knock.
Who's there?
You.
You who?
That's *my* line!

To pray this week

Lord God, here I am, ready to do whatever you need me to.

PROPER 9

Sunday between 3 and 9 July inclusive

Thought for the day

In Christ we become a new creation.

Readings

2 Kings 5:1-14 or Isaiah 66:10-14
Psalm 30 or Psalm 66:1-9
Galatians 6:(1-6) 7-16
Luke 10:1-11, 16-20

Aim

To hear about the seventy being sent out by Jesus.

Starter

Send people out in pairs with matchboxes, on a mission to collect six different things which fit in their box. Show one another the results when everyone gets back. You can make this a timed activity if your schedule is tight.

Teaching

First fill in the background to this mission. Jesus began by doing the teaching and healing all over the local area, training his followers or disciples as he went. Jesus realises that there are huge numbers of people all ready to hear the good news, but only a few people to teach them. He talks about it as being like a huge harvest of people, ripe to gather in, but with very few workers to do it. So now he spreads the net wider, by sending out seventy-two of his trained followers. As this is quite a large number to visualise, have seventy-two paper people cut out and spread them all over the floor in the middle of the circle. Let a few children put them into pairs, because Jesus sent these people out in pairs. They can discuss the advantages of this.

Jesus gathered this crowd of people together and gave them their instructions. Have these written out on a large sheet of paper or length of wallpaper:

1. Be careful.
2. Travel light.
3. Don't waste time chatting on the way.
4. 'Peace to this house!'
5. Eat what you are given.
6. Heal the sick in body and mind.
7. Tell them the kingdom of God is very close to them.

Use the instruction list on the worksheet with its picture symbols as you tell the children what happened, and how excited they were when they got back because of the many ways God had blessed their work.

Praying

Lord, so many people
have no idea of how happy they could be
with you at the centre of their life.
Please send us lots more workers
into this harvest,
to let the people know about you
and bring them safely into your kingdom. Amen.

Activities

Using the cut-out people and a large sheet of paper, make a collage picture of this mission, sticking on the children's drawings of roads, villages, trees and the people hearing the good news everywhere, and being healed. The worksheet has some follow-up to the story of Naaman, as well as a copy of the list of instructions given to the seventy-two.

Notes

INSTRUCTIONS

1 Be careful

2 Travel light

3 Don't waste time chatting on the way

4 'Peace to this house!'

5 Eat what you are given

6 Heal the sick in body and mind

7 Tell them the kingdom of God is very close to them

MATHS

How many?

...instructions? ☐

...workers sent out? ☐

...pairs of workers? ☐

...times was Naaman told to wash? ☐

TOTAL LOTS!

(And that's how many more workers are needed LOTS!)

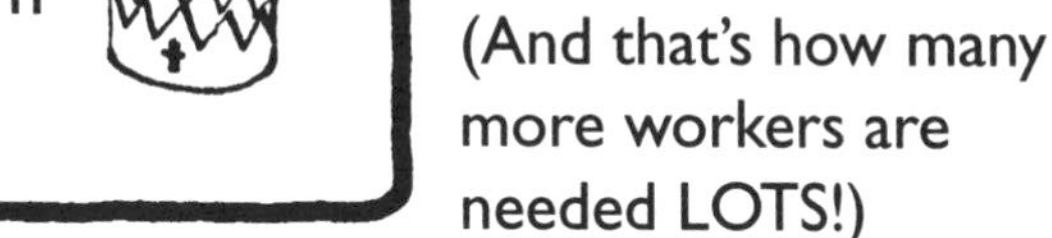

This is _ _ _ _ _ _ _ .The prophet _ _ _ _ _ _ _ has told him to wash _ _ _ _ _ _ times in the river _ _ _ _ _ _ _ to get rid of his _ _ _ _ _ _ _ _ . Does it work? Yes/No

Read the story in 2 Kings 5:1-14

To pray this week

Lord, so many people have no idea of how happy they could be with you at the centre of their life. Please send us lots more workers into this harvest, to let the people know about you and bring them safely into your kingdom.

Amen.

Who do you know, who is working on God's harvest?
Write their names here. Pray for them.

How would you feel about living like this?

PROPER 10

Sunday between 10 and 16 July inclusive

Thought for the day

Straighten your lives out and live by God's standards of love.

Readings

Amos 7:7-17 or Deuteronomy 30:9-14
Psalm 82 or Psalm 25:1-10
Colossians 1:1-14
Luke 10:25-37

Aim

To think about measuring our lives against God's plumb line.

Starter

Have some tape measures and get the children measuring each other and recording the results on a length of string to see how far our Rocks group would stretch if we put them end to end.

Teaching

It's amazing what you discover when you start measuring! Explain that today we're going to look at another kind of measure. We now know how we measure up in metres and centimetres, but what about God's measuring stick of love? Introduce the children to Amos, who has come to tell us about something God showed him. What was it, Amos?

Amos greets the children and tells them he comes from the southern part of Israel. He could see that the people in the northern part were treating their poor people really unfairly, and not caring about anyone who wasn't able to earn lots of money. And they were not bothering to worship the true God either; they were playing around with other things they called gods. He shows the children a plumb line and asks them if they know what it is. He tells them how God showed him a crooked wall, and he was able to measure the wall against the straight vertical of the plumb line and check whether it was straight or not. And he had found that the people of Israel were like a crooked wall against God's plumb line of fair treatment, loving care and respect for everyone, however poor.

Amos was the one God asked to go and tell the people that their lives and their country needed straightening out, and fast! But they didn't listen to him. They just got angry with him.

Thank Amos for coming, and ask him to remind them of what God's plumb line is, so we can measure ourselves against it and check whether we're straight and level enough. Amos tells them: 'Love the Lord your God with all your heart and with all your mind and with all your strength. And love your neighbour as yourself.'

You can all sing this with actions to remind you, to the tune of *London's burning*:

You shall love the Lord your God with
all your heart and all your mind and
all your strength! All your strength!
And love your neighbour,
and love your neighbour.

Praying

Lord God,
help me to notice
when other people need my help,
and remind me to do
what I can to help them. Amen.

Activities

There are instructions on the worksheet for making their own plumb lines and spirit levels, which can be labelled with the summary of the Law. They will each need a plastic bottle and a small weight of some kind. There is also a drawing activity to remind the children of the story of the good neighbour, and the Bible reference for this.

Notes

How to make a plumb line and a spirit level. You will need

a clean plastic bottle

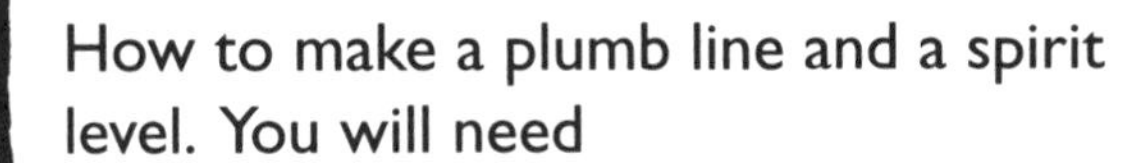

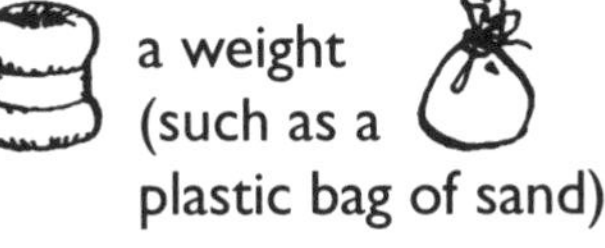

water

sticky tape

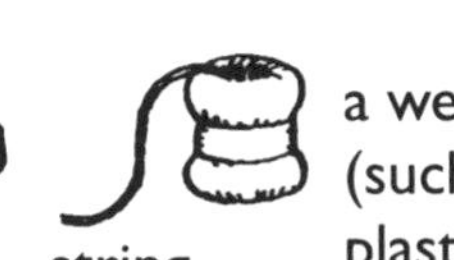

string

a weight (such as a plastic bag of sand)

The plumb line
'Plumb' means lead, which is heavy. Fix your heavy weight, or 'plumb', on to a piece of string, about 0.5m long.

The spirit level
These used to be filled with white spirit, but water works fine. Fill the bottle with water so there is a small bubble of air left at the top. Close it tightly. Use tape to mark where the bubble is on a level surface.

How you use them

The plumb line
To check if a wall has been built straight, hang your plumb line against it. If the wall is straight, the plumb line is the same distance from the wall all the way down. If the wall slopes, you will notice as the plumb line always hangs straight.

The spirit level
To check if the top of a wall is level, lay the bottle on it and see where the bubble lies. If the wall slopes the bubble will be off-centre.

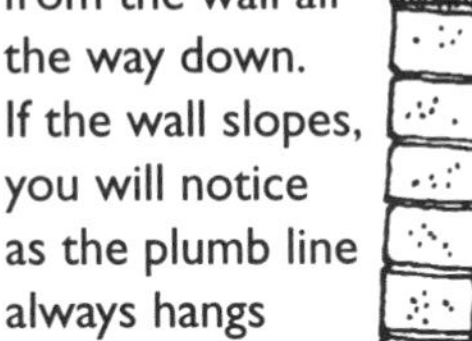

Amos told the people

lives

'Your

out!'

need

straightening

How do our lives measure up? Are they straight and true like good walls? or are they leaning to selfishness here and there?

A traveller was mugged and left for dead. Respectable people took no notice of him. They walked by on the other side of the road.

A Samaritan saw him, went over and gave him first aid. Then he looked after him, took him on his donkey to an inn and paid for him to be cared for till he recovered.
Luke 10:25-37

To pray this week

Lord God, help me to notice when other people need my help, and remind me to do what I can to help them. Amen.

PROPER 11

Sunday between 17 and 23 July inclusive

Thought for the day

Against impossible odds God has reconciled us to himself, in Christ.

Readings

Amos 8:1-12 or Genesis 18:1-10a
Psalm 52 or Psalm 15
Colossians 1:15-28
Luke 10:38-42

Aim

To look at the importance of listening to God.

Starter

Sit in a circle, with one blindfolded person in the centre. Another person creeps round the outside of the circle with a jangly set of keys. The blindfolded person points to where the person has got to. If they are right they take the keys and a new person is blindfolded.

Teaching

Begin with a sketch to express the busy nature of our lives. It will need to be prepared beforehand using one or two of the children. An alarm clock rings and the children dash in with dressing-gowns and teddies. They pretend to eat their breakfast really quickly, and grab books and pencil-case for school. They dash back in for lunch-boxes, and out, back for football kit or equivalent, and out, back for swimming gear, and out, back for violin or equivalent, and out, back to sit and watch television and eat something, and out, in wearing dressing-gowns and teddies again, and out.

Talk about what the children do on each day of the week and how nice it is to be able to do all these things, but how important it is to stop and spend quiet times every day with God. Have the children acting out the Martha and Mary story, bringing out the need to get the listening times right so that all the practical doing falls properly into place.

Praying

Here I am, Lord.
I have come to spend some time with you,
to sit at your feet and be quiet with you.

Activities

There are instructions on the worksheet for making a prayer corner for their bedroom, to be used as a reminder for daily prayer and a focus for them. There is also a prayer pattern using a hand drawing, which can be cut out and stuck on to the prayer corner.

Notes

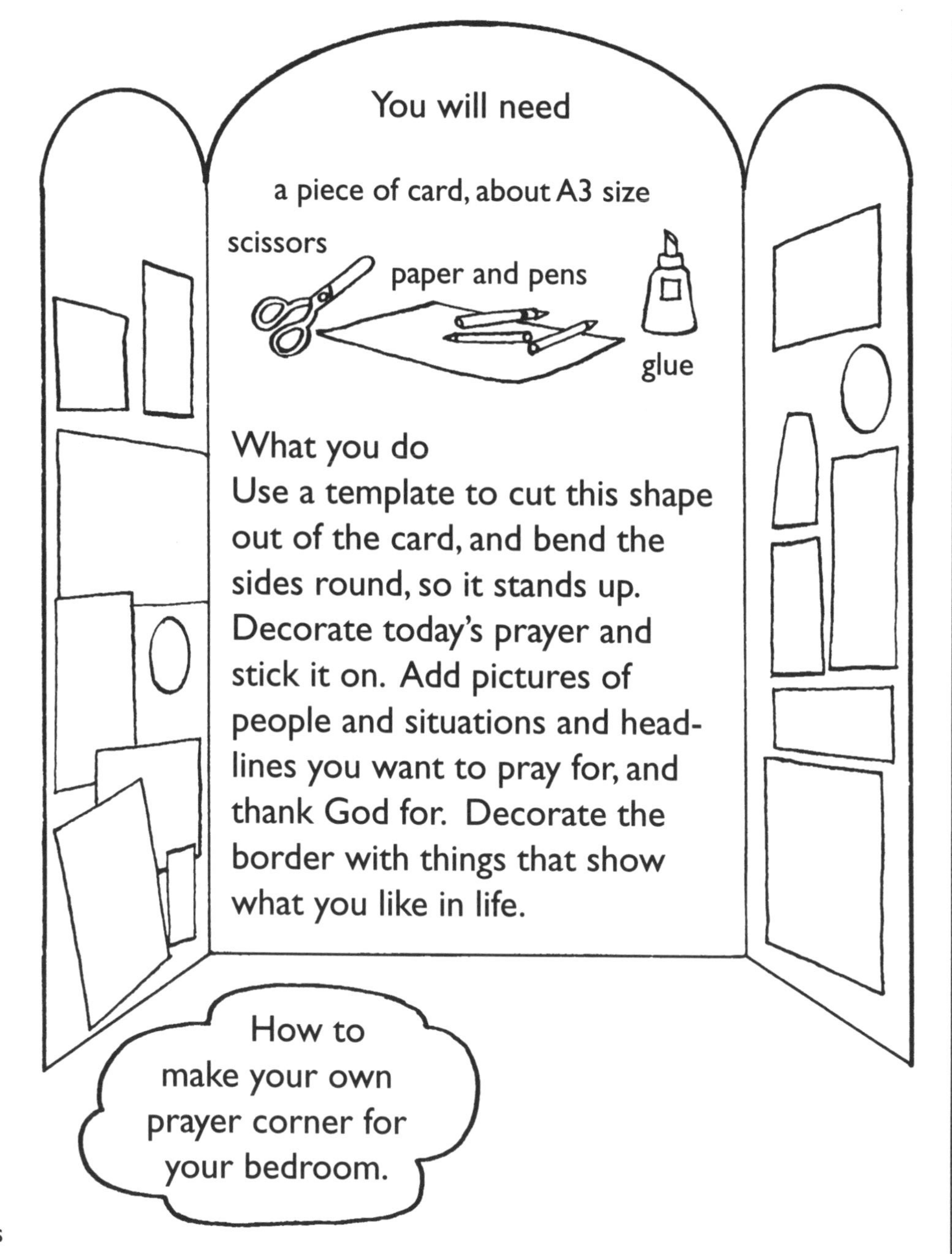

Here I am, Lord.
I have come to spend some time with you, to sit at your feet and be quiet with you.

1 2 3 4 5 L or R 5 4 3 2 1

Label each finger like this:

1 Pray for people with power over others
2 Pray for our leaders and teachers
3 Thank God for all the good things
4 Pray for family and friends
5 Pray for yourself and your needs

PROPER 12

Sunday between 24 and 30 July inclusive

Thought for the day

Keep asking for God's Spirit and he will keep pouring out his blessing on you.

Readings

Hosea 1:2-10 or Genesis 18:20-32
Psalm 85 or Psalm 138
Colossians 2:6-15 (16-19)
Luke 11:1-13

Aim

To look at the meaning of the Lord's prayer.

Starter

Play a game of hide and seek, or sardines, or look for a hidden object, with clues of 'hotter' or 'colder' only being given if they are asked for.

Teaching

Jesus often used to go off on his own to talk things over with his Father in heaven and listen to his Father's advice. Sometimes they would just be quiet in one another's company. These times helped Jesus have the wisdom and energy he needed to do his work, as we mentioned last week.

His followers could see how useful those times were to Jesus, and they wanted to do it themselves but they didn't know how to. So they asked Jesus to teach them all how to pray. And this is what Jesus suggested they did.

1. Remember that God is your Father in heaven, and that he is holy.
2. Ask for the kingdom of God to come, and God's will to be done.
3. Ask for enough to eat and for your needs for the day.
4. Ask God to forgive your sins, just as you have forgiven people who have upset you.
5. Ask God to lead you safely through temptation and out of evil.

Have them written up on separate cards, and answer any questions about each one as you go along. Jumble them up and invite a couple of children to put them in the right order again. Then have someone reading each one out, and a pause for everyone to do what the card says. Introducing them to the meaning like this, before the traditional words, will prevent understanding being blocked by familiar but undigested words.

Now see if any of them know the traditional form of this teaching, known as the Lord's Prayer. Teach them these actions to do as they say it, to make sure they are praying, and not just reciting some instructions.

Our Father
in heaven,
hallowed be your name.
Your kingdom come, (Look down)
your will be done on earth
as it is in heaven. (look up)
Give us today our daily bread (cup hands)
and forgive us our sins
as we forgive those
who sin against us.
Lead us not into temptation
but deliver us from evil.
For the kingdom, the power
and the glory are yours,
now and for ever. Amen. (Move arms slowly upwards and raise heads at the same time)

Praying

Use the Lord's Prayer with actions.

Activities

The instructions are written on the sheet so that they can be coloured, decorated and stuck on to the prayer corner made last week. There is also an activity looking at giving and gifts.

Notes

Teach us to pray

1 Remember that God is your Father in heaven, and that he is holy.

2 Ask for the kingdom of God to come, and God's will to be done.

3 Ask for enough to eat and for your needs for the day.

4 Ask God to forgive your sins, just as you have forgiven people who have upset you.

5 Ask God to lead you safely through temptation and out of evil.

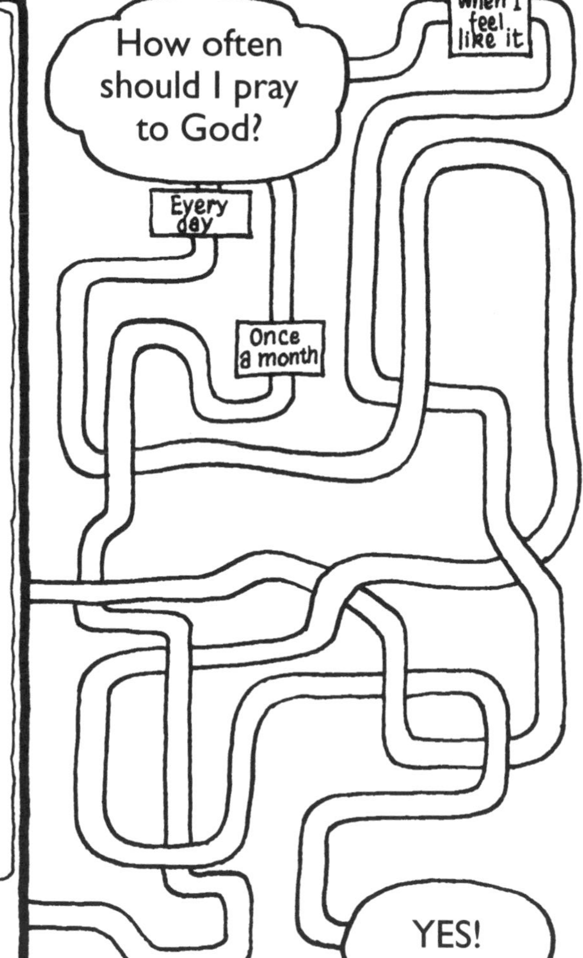

Can you 'seek' the answer?

Knock knock!
Who's there?
Ivan.
Ivan who?
Ivan unexpected guest and we need some bread!

What on earth is he wanting? (Luke 11:1-13)

To pray this week

Our Father in heaven,
hallowed be your name.
Your kingdom come,
your will be done on earth
as it is in heaven.
Give us today our daily bread
and forgive us our sins as we
forgive those who sin against us.
Lead us not into temptation but
deliver us from evil. For the kingdom,
the power and the glory are yours,
now and for ever. Amen.

Proper 13

Sunday between 31 July and 6 August inclusive

Thought for the day

True richness is not material wealth; true security is not a financial matter.

Readings

Hosea 11:1-11 or Ecclesiastes 1:2, 12-14; 2:18-23
Psalm 107:1-9, 43 or Psalm 49:1-12
Colossians 3:1-11
Luke 12:13-21

Aim

To look at real lasting wealth.

Starter

My aunt went to Paris. Sit in a circle. The first person says, 'My aunt went to Paris and she bought a . . .' They name something and mime it at the same time. The next person has to say this item followed by their own, and so on.

Teaching

Have a tape recording of excerpts from several current TV advertisements, and they can guess what item is being advertised. Point out that the fact we know these means that the adverts are working. Although this is good for the company who makes the chocolate or car, it can encourage us to be greedy, and discontented.

Show the children a timeline with 'Now' at the left end, an ongoing arrow at the right end and a point marked 'Death' about a third of the way along the line. Remind the children that our new life in Christ doesn't stop at death, but goes on for ever in heaven. The bit on earth here is only quite a short section of our whole life.

Lots of people put their trust in money and things, rather than in God. They forget that these can only last up to death, at the very most. If they've spent no time getting the long-lasting spiritual treasure, then they're going to have to spend an awfully long time without anything.

Tell the story of the rich fool, using the script below.

Music from Beethoven's *Pastoral Symphony* fades in.

Narrator There was once a rich man who had a very good harvest.
(Sound of running)

Slave Master! Master!

Rich man *(Snoring; wakes up)* Oh! Yes – what is it, slave?

Slave Master, we've filled all the barns with the crops but there's still lots more left to store.

Rich man *(Laughs)* Well, well! Such a good harvest that there's no room to store my crops, eh? Now what can I do about that, I wonder.

Slave Perhaps you could give some away?

Rich man What! Good heavens, no! I know what I'll do. Slave – start pulling the barns down.

Slave Pull them down, Master? B . . . b . . . but we've only just filled them up.

Rich man Then empty them, you fool! We're going to build *enormous* barns – enough to hold all my grain.

Slave Very well, Master; your wish is my command. *(Runs off. His voice is heard in the distance)* Come on, lads, get busy. All the grain is to be moved.

Other slaves *(Groaning)* Oh no! What on earth for? After all that work, etc.
(Sounds of workers pouring grain fades into music. Music fades into building sounds.)

Slave driver Come on there, stop wasting time.
(Sound of whip)

Rich man Ah, good, the new barns are splendid! Keep up the good work. *(Music fades in)* Now I've got so much grain I can enjoy myself for years to come. I think I'll start with a feast. No more worries for me!
(Sounds of eating and drinking)
(Cymbal, or saucepan lids)

God Fool! Fool! *(Cymbal)*

Rich man *(Flustered)* Eh? Oh, my goodness, who said that?
(Cymbal)

God I, God, tell you that you are a fool! This very night you are going to die. What use will your hoard of grain be to you then? *(Cymbal)* What use will your hoard of grain be to you then?
(Music fades in to finish)

Narrator So the man saw that getting rich did not make him safe and secure.

Praying

Thank you, Father,
for showing us a new way to live,
trusting in your love
and building treasure in heaven.

Activities

On the worksheet there is an activity to help them weigh up the better bargain: being rich or being loved – being happy because you've just bought a CD or being happy because you know God loves you? They will need Bibles to look up the reference in Hosea. Try making the script into a radio play, with sound effects. It could then be used for a parish Bible study.

Draw a cartoon strip story called 'The foolish lottery winner'

Winning	Spending	?

Being rich

Being loved

Which is worth more?

Being happy because you know God loves you

Being happy because you have bought a CD

Which is going to last longest?

To pray this week

Thank you, Father, for showing us a new way to live, trusting in your love and building treasure in heaven.

What's this for?

and this?

God says

Hosea 11

Proper 14

Sunday between 7 and 13 August inclusive

Thought for the day

Have faith in God, and get yourself ready to meet him.

Readings

Isaiah 1:1, 10-20
Psalm 50:1-8, 22-23
Hebrews 11:1-3, 8-16
Luke 12:32-40

Aim

To know the importance of keeping ready.

Starter

'What's the time, Mr Wolf?' or a similar 'creeping-up' kind of game. Talk about the way you had to keep alert because you didn't know exactly when you were going to have to run, or when Mr Wolf would turn round.

Teaching

Remind the children that after Jesus died and rose again he went to live in heaven. (Let them tell you, if they know.) But one day he will come back, and he hopes that we'll still be watchful and ready for him when he comes.

How do people keep themselves prepared for helping at accidents? They learn first aid and they practise so they don't forget. How do we make sure we're prepared for a cycling test? We learn how to cycle safely and then practise. What about being prepared for Jesus – how can we do that? It's the same; we need to learn how to live his way and then keep practising. Point out that they are all learning week by week when they come to Living Stones, and when they read the Bible. They practise all through the week, doing their praying, and choosing how to behave. Sometimes we get it wrong, but the important thing is to keep trying.

Get some of the children to act out the parables of the master finding the faithful servants and waiting on them for a change, and the burglars not being able to rob the house because the owner is being very tiresome and keeping watch.

Praying

Lord Jesus,
I want you to find me
watching faithfully
when you come again. Amen.

Activities

On the worksheet there is a picture to colour of fire-fighters getting ready to rush to a fire. The quiz linked to it can be used to start discussion about our spiritual readiness. There is a cartoon to draw to reinforce the teaching, and an activity which requires Bibles so they can look up Isaiah references.

Notes

Ready and waiting!

Who is getting ready here?

nurses	
firefighters	
soldiers	

Where are they off to?

a shipwreck	
a party	
a fire	

How do they know what to do?

they're in training	
they don't know	
they watched Fireman Sam	

To pray this week

Lord Jesus,
I want you to find me
watching faithfully
when you come again.
Amen.

This is a burglar being caught by the owner of the house

Isaiah 1:16-17

T_ _ _ your _ _ _ _ _ deeds
out _ _ my s _ _ _ _ _!

S _ _ _ doing w _ _ _ _ _

l _ _ _ n to do r _ _ _ _ _!

S _ _ k j _ _ t _ _ e!

e _ c _ _ r _ _ _
t _ _ opp _ _ _ _ _ _ d

D _ f _ _ d the cause of
_ _ _ f _ _ _ _ _ _ l _ _ s

pl _ _ _ the cause _ _ the
w _ d _ w

Proper 15

Sunday between 14 and 20 August inclusive

Thought for the day

When we fix our eyes on Jesus our lives will reflect his nature.

Readings

Isaiah 5:1-7 or Jeremiah 23:23-29
Psalm 80:1-2, 8-19 or Psalm 82
Hebrews 11:29-12:2
Luke 12:49-56

Aim

To learn about fixing our eyes on Jesus and running the race unhindered.

Starter

Loads of fun. This team game involves the first team member running up to a point, collecting a heavy bag and lugging it back to the team. The second team member lugs it back, dumps it and runs back. The next collects it, and so on. The team with most luggage journeys logged in the time allocated wins.

Teaching

Point out how much everyone was slowed down by the weight of the luggage, and also how much easier it is to run to the right place if we look where we're going.

Bring out an envelope (stamped and franked) and explain how some of the early Christian leaders wrote letters to keep in touch with the churches. The Bible has collected some of these old letters, written nearly two thousand years ago, so that we can still read them today. So this letter (not the actual envelope, though!) has been around a very long time. We're not even sure who wrote it, but it's got such useful hints in it that it's well worth reading.

Take out the letter, and read the first introductory section to Hebrews, followed by the *International Children's Bible* (New Century) version of today's reading. Draw attention to how it fits in with what we found in our game, about running light and fixing our eyes on Jesus.

Talk about people who can't enjoy what they've got because they're always wishing they had something better or different, and it turns them into unhappy moaners. God wants them to be free of the 'wanting' so they can enjoy life whatever they have or haven't got.

Talk about people who want to boss their friends around all the time, and end up without friends or with people scared of them. Their bossiness and bullying is like a heavy bag they're carrying, and it stops them really enjoying life. God wants them to put it down so they can play with other children and be happy.

If we are carrying any habits like moaning or bossiness, or keeping an enemy or winding someone up all the time, the writer of this letter from the Roman world is saying, 'Why don't you put that down today, and fix your eyes on Jesus, so you can live free and happy?'

Praying

Lord Jesus,
I'm going to run the race
with my eyes
fixed on you.
And if I get cluttered
with silly or bad habits,
please remind me
to put them down
so I can run free. Amen.

Activities

On the worksheet there are instructions for making a race game. It requires two fridge magnets for each child.

Notes

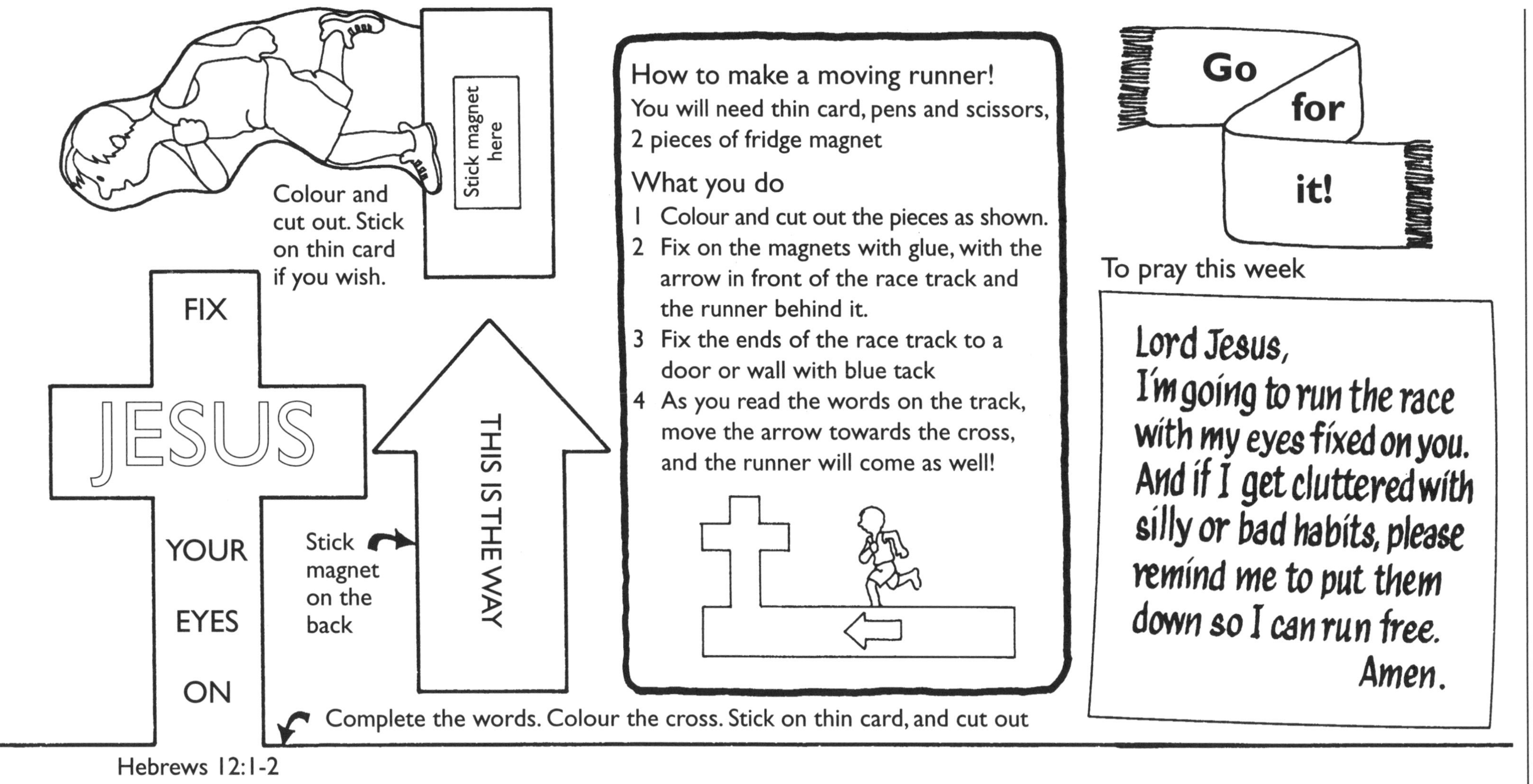

How to make a moving runner!

You will need thin card, pens and scissors, 2 pieces of fridge magnet

What you do

1. Colour and cut out the pieces as shown.
2. Fix on the magnets with glue, with the arrow in front of the race track and the runner behind it.
3. Fix the ends of the race track to a door or wall with blue tack
4. As you read the words on the track, move the arrow towards the cross, and the runner will come as well!

To pray this week

Lord Jesus,
I'm going to run the race with my eyes fixed on you. And if I get cluttered with silly or bad habits, please remind me to put them down so I can run free.
Amen.

Complete the words. Colour the cross. Stick on thin card, and cut out

Hebrews 12:1-2

LET US _ _ _ _ _ OFF EVERYTHING THAT _ _ _ _ _ _ _ _ AND THE _ _ _ THAT EASILY _ _ _ _ _ _ _ _ _ _ _ US, AND RUN THE _ _ _ _ . LET US _ _ _ OUR EYES _ _ _ _ _ _ _ _ .

PROPER 16

Sunday between 21 and 27 August inclusive

Thought for the day

God sets his leaders apart to challenge prejudices and assumptions, and alert people to the truth.

Readings

Jeremiah 1:4-10 or Isaiah 58:9b-14
Psalm 71:1-6 or Psalm 103:1-8
Hebrews 12:18-29
Luke 13:10-17

Aim

To know the story of the crippled woman being healed on the Sabbath.

Starter

Use a beanbag or soft ball and make a circle with one person in the centre. They throw the beanbag to each person in turn and have it thrown back to them. After six throws they change with the person they would have thrown to next. Everyone shouts in time to the throwing: 'One, Sunday; two, Monday; three, Tuesday; four, Wednesday; five, Thursday; six, Friday; seven, Saturday, the Sabbath, all change!'

Teaching

Remind the children of the fourth Commandment – to keep the Sabbath, or seventh day of the week, special and holy, and rest on that day, because it was on the seventh day that God rested from his work of creation.

See if they have any ideas about why we now keep the first day of the week special and holy, instead of the seventh, and tell them how the Jewish religion still celebrates Saturday, the Sabbath. What would they think it meant not to work on the Sabbath? What kind of work would people still have to do? Jot the ideas down in two columns – headed with a tick and a cross. Amongst the obvious 'work' tasks suggest things like preparing food, leading your animals to have a drink, putting out a fire, and rescuing your donkey if it fell into a ditch, so the children can discuss them and decide whether they should be counted as work or not.

Now that they have a taste of the way the Jewish leaders had tried to sort out what the Commandment meant, and can see that if you get too picky you lose sight of what it's really about, tell the story of what happened on one Sabbath day when Jesus was worshipping at the local synagogue. Involve the children in acting it out as you tell the story, and have another leader getting annoyed by the healing and telling everyone not to come for healing on the Sabbath.

Freeze the story there and ask the children what they think. Was this leader right? Was it wrong to heal on the Sabbath? Or was the Sabbath a good day to heal on? After they've said their thoughts, one by one, without comment from you (except encouraging acknowledgement), carry on with the story, and tell them how Jesus reacted to the leader's attitude.

Praying

Thank you, Lord God,
for showing us how to be free.
Teach us to notice the needs
of those around us
and make us ready to help. Amen.

Activities

On the worksheet there are instructions for making a week of daily thoughts in a slider, which can be fixed on the children's prayer corners at home. There are also Bible study puzzles to reinforce the questions raised by today's Gospel reading.

Notes

God loves to

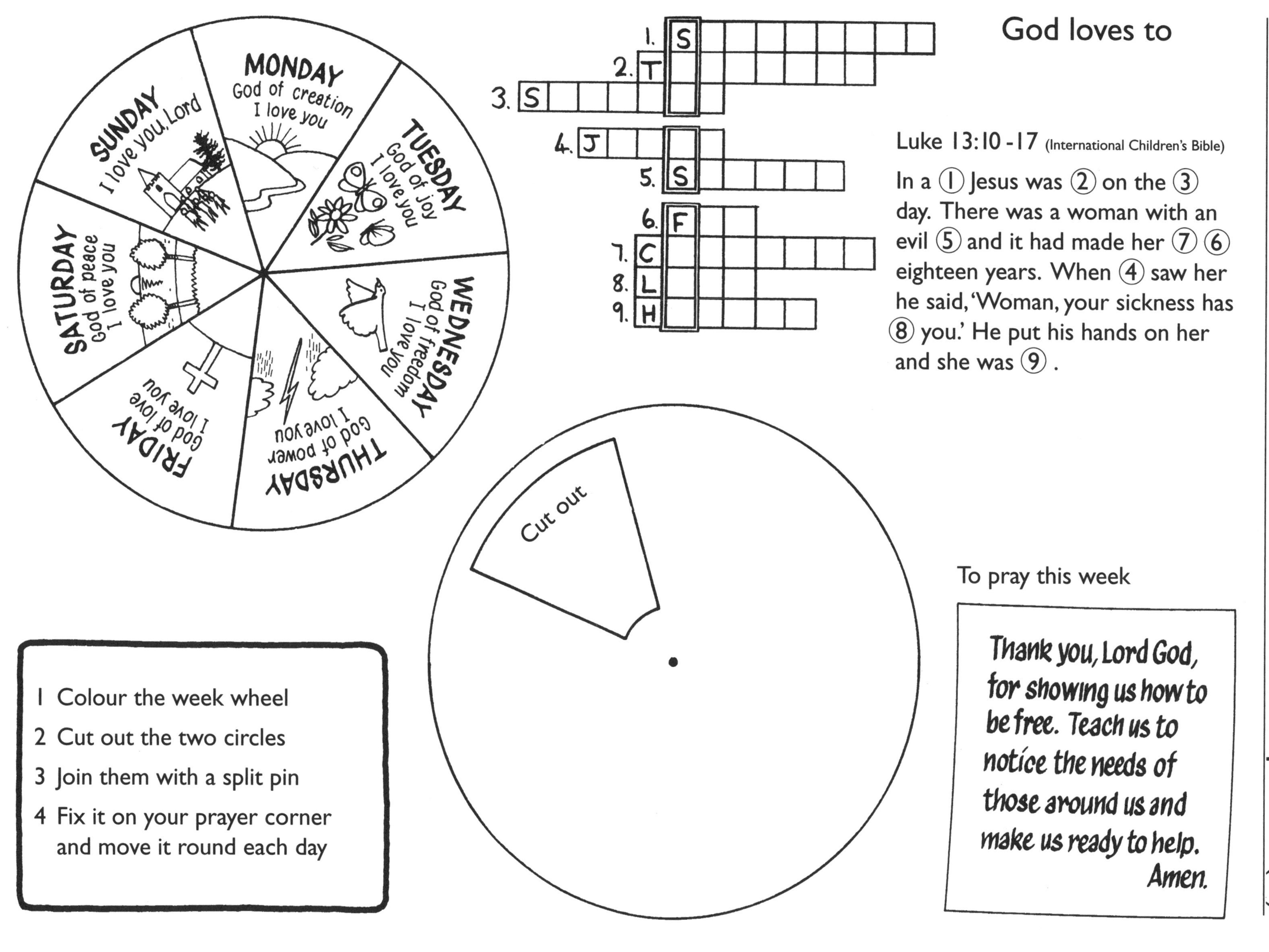

Luke 13:10-17 (International Children's Bible)

In a ① Jesus was ② on the ③ day. There was a woman with an evil ⑤ and it had made her ⑦ ⑥ eighteen years. When ④ saw her he said, 'Woman, your sickness has ⑧ you.' He put his hands on her and she was ⑨ .

To pray this week

Thank you, Lord God, for showing us how to be free. Teach us to notice the needs of those around us and make us ready to help. Amen.

1 Colour the week wheel
2 Cut out the two circles
3 Join them with a split pin
4 Fix it on your prayer corner and move it round each day

Proper 17

Sunday between 28 August and 3 September inclusive

Thought for the day

When we live God's way, both individually and as a community, we will be greatly blessed.

Readings

Jeremiah 2:4-13 or Ecclesiasticus 10:12-18
Psalm 81:1, 10-16 or Psalm 112
Hebrews 13:1-8, 15-16
Luke 14:1, 7-14

Aim

To look at the implications of Jesus' teaching about hospitality.

Starter

In pairs feed one another jelly or creamed rice pudding. Provide clothing protection!

Teaching

Beforehand prepare two children to act out the guests at the party who are taking the top and bottom seats, and have to swap round when the host wants the lower one up at the top.

Talk about the way we usually feed ourselves when we're hungry, and give ourselves drinks when we're thirsty. When we were feeding one another we got an idea of what it's like to look after someone else, checking that they have caught the spoonful, and don't have drips down their chin.

Thinking of other people's needs is an important part of the Christian way of living. One day Jesus was invited out to lunch, and he noticed the pushy way some of the guests were making sure they had the best seats, nearest the food and drink and near the hosts, so sitting there would make them look important. Jesus didn't like what he saw. It made him sad that people were pushy like this, wanting to be more important than anyone else, and not thinking of other people's feelings. So he told them this story to help them understand a better way of living.

Now ask the children to perform the sketch they have prepared, with the rest of the children being the rest of the guests. Draw out the point Jesus was making about wrong values – being thought of as important shouldn't matter to us nearly as much as it often does. As Christians we are not to think, 'What's in this for me?' all the time.

Praying

Jesus, teach me to give
and not to count the cost,
to toil and not to seek for rest,
to work and not to ask for any reward
except the reward of knowing
I am doing your will. Amen.

Activities

The worksheet encourages the children to look at the second part of today's teaching, dealing with our hospitality with no strings attached. There are also recipes and suggestions for staging a party, with an invitation format, so that they can put the teaching straight into practice as part of your parish outreach programme.

Notes

Why not throw a party?

Dear ....
Please will you come to
a party at ....
on ...., held at
....
Love from
.... RSVP

Banana milkshake

You will need

- a banana
- half a pint of milk
- teaspoon of runny honey

What you do

Peel and chop the banana.
Put everything in a screw-top jar.
Shake it lots.
Pour into a glass.

PARTY TIME

dips and dishes
yoghurt, mayonnaise and chopped chives
sticks of carrot and cucumber
hollow pepper

pizza faces
tomato
sliced olives
sliced red pepper
cheese
peppers

crunchies
cornflakes stuck together with chocolate

dice cakes
chocolate pieces and a slab of cake cut up and covered in white icing

*A useful, brilliant book is:
The simply wonderful cookbook (Lion) by Heather Robinson

To pray this week

Jesus, teach me to give and not to count the cost, to toil and not to seek for rest, to work and not to ask for any reward except the reward of knowing I am doing your will.
Amen.

Proper 18

Sunday between 4 and 10 September inclusive

Thought for the day

Following Jesus is expensive – it costs everything, but it's worth it.

Readings

Jeremiah 18:1-11 or Deuteronomy 30:15-20
Psalm 139:1-6,13-18 or Psalm 1
Philemon 1-21
Luke 14:25-33

Aim

To look at what it costs to follow Jesus.

Starter

Tower building. Collect lots of boxes and cartons, and sort them into sizes with price tags on them. Use Monopoly money and make the prices of the 'bricks' very high, so the children are dealing in hundreds of pounds. Issue each small group with a set amount of money and have a leader in charge of the brickyard. The members of the teams have to decide which bricks to buy with their money to stack up their tower. (No sticky tape allowed!)

Teaching

Use two leaders or a leader and a child to tell the story as a conversation, something like this:

Miriam is sweeping the floor when Alex comes bursting in.

Alex Miriam! Miriam! Where are you? Oh, there you are!

Miriam Now, mind where you put the dust from those sandals, Alex. I've just swept over there!

Alex Oh, yes . . . sorry, dear. But listen, I've had a *really* good idea.

Miriam Not another one already! I was cleaning up after your last good idea for days.

Alex Ah, the olive tree shaker, you mean. Well, I wasn't to know the olives and insects would all shake off into your bowl of flour, was I! Anyway, this idea is different, and it's *really good.*

Miriam OK, dear, I'm listening. You do have some very good ideas, I know. You just need someone like me to stop you getting carried away, sometimes. Tell me your idea.

Alex A tower.

Miriam A tower? What do you mean, a tower?

Alex I'm going to build one! It'll be very high, so you'll be able to climb up the tower and check on all the sheep and lambs without having to go all the way to the fields! There, what do you think?

Miriam Mmm, it sounds like a good time-saver. I could sit at the top of your tower and sunbathe in between looking at the sheep, couldn't I?

Alex Yes, Miriam, you could.

Miriam There's one rather big problem though.

Alex Oh, really? What's that, Miriam?

Miriam Money. Bricks cost money, and we haven't got any spare money that I know of. How are you going to pay for it?

Alex Well, I've got enough bricks to build the first bit, Miriam.

Miriam Oh, Alex, you'll look a prize idiot if you build the first bit and then can't finish it off! All the neighbours would tease you about it for years.

Alex Yes, I suppose you're right. Perhaps I'll go and sit under the olive tree before supper and work out a few sums.

Miriam It's chicken soup and matzos, and I'll need some help!

Then read Luke 14:28-30, 33. If we decide to join Cubs or Brownies, or start a new sport or learn to play the flute, we know we are committing ourselves. We know our choice will take up time, and we won't be able to do some other things.

Following Jesus is a commitment, too. We have to be prepared to work at telling the truth, or getting on with people we find hard, or standing up for what is right even when we get teased for it. We can't follow Jesus and go on winding everyone up and cheating and lying as if nothing has changed. We have to be prepared to put down those bad habits we have got into and Jesus will help us in that. We have to be ready to go wherever Jesus leads us; and that could be anywhere.

Praying

Lord, even before I say a word,
you already know what I am going to say.
You are all around me – in front and at the back.
You have put your hand on me.
Your knowledge is amazing to me.
It is more than I can understand.
(From Psalm 139)

Activities

There is a cost-counting puzzle on the worksheet, and the instructions for making a reversible cross which looks at the cost and the benefits of following Christ.

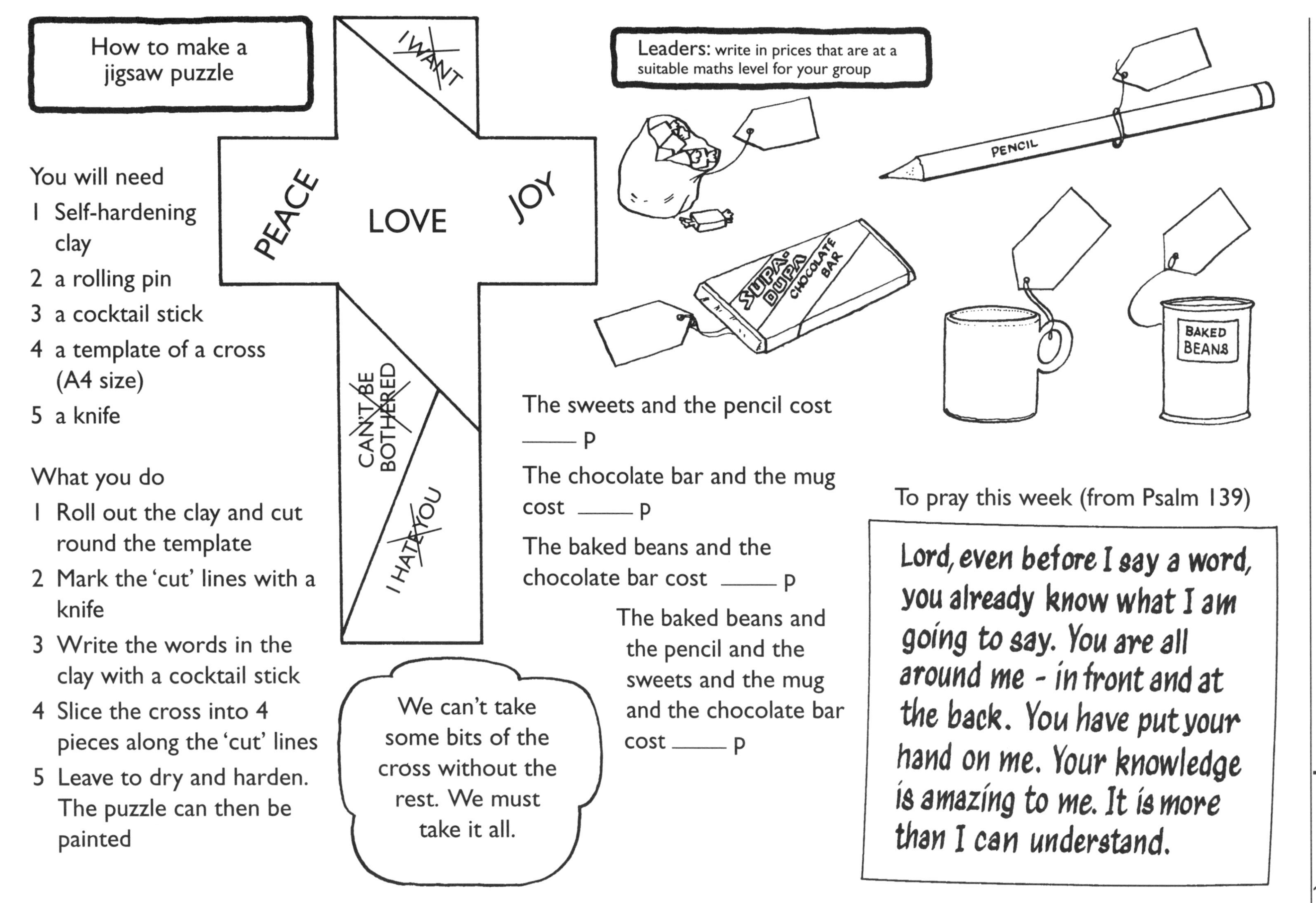
How to make a jigsaw puzzle
You will need
1 Self-hardening clay
2 a rolling pin
3 a cocktail stick
4 a template of a cross (A4 size)
5 a knife
What you do
1 Roll out the clay and cut round the template
2 Mark the 'cut' lines with a knife
3 Write the words in the clay with a cocktail stick
4 Slice the cross into 4 pieces along the 'cut' lines
5 Leave to dry and harden. The puzzle can then be painted
I WANT
PEACE
LOVE
JOY
CAN'T BE BOTHERED
I HATE YOU
We can't take some bits of the cross without the rest. We must take it all.
Leaders: write in prices that are at a suitable maths level for your group
PENCIL
SUPA DUPA CHOCOLATE BAR
BAKED BEANS
The sweets and the pencil cost ____ p
The chocolate bar and the mug cost ____ p
The baked beans and the chocolate bar cost ____ p
The baked beans and the pencil and the sweets and the mug and the chocolate bar cost ____ p
To pray this week (from Psalm 139)
Lord, even before I say a word, you already know what I am going to say. You are all around me – in front and at the back. You have put your hand on me. Your knowledge is amazing to me. It is more than I can understand.

Proper 19

Sunday between 11 and 17 September inclusive

Thought for the day

Jesus does not avoid the company of sinners but befriends them.

Readings

Jeremiah 4:11-12, 22-28 or Exodus 32:7-14
Psalm 14 or Psalm 51:1-10
1 Timothy 1:12-17
Luke 15:1-10

Aim

To explore the meaning of the lost sheep and the lost coin.

Starter

Hunt the coins. For larger groups, have several coins on the go at the same time.

Teaching

Share your stories of losing something really important and then finding it again after searching everywhere for it. (Or you could pretend to have lost something and get everyone searching for it. When it is found you can draw attention to the relief and happiness.)

Jesus knew what this was like. Perhaps it was his mum or auntie who had once lost one of those coins from a marriage necklace, and he remembered the way they had all searched and celebrated.

Show the children a picture of such a necklace, or, if possible, a real example borrowed from your local Resource centre, and tell the story of the woman losing one of the coins. Use a real broom as you describe the sweeping of the whole house.

Explain that whenever one of us gets 'lost' – cut off from God – he too is really sad, and keeps searching and searching until he finds us again.

Praying

We pray for those
who have made wrong choices
and cut themselves off from God.
We pray for all those
who are living evil lives.
May all the lost be found again. Amen.

Activities

There are instructions on the worksheet for making a marriage necklace and a sheep, and a puzzle to reinforce the two stories of the sheep and the coin.

Notes

How to make a headband dowry of shiny coins

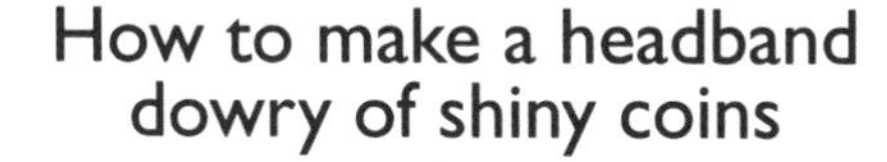

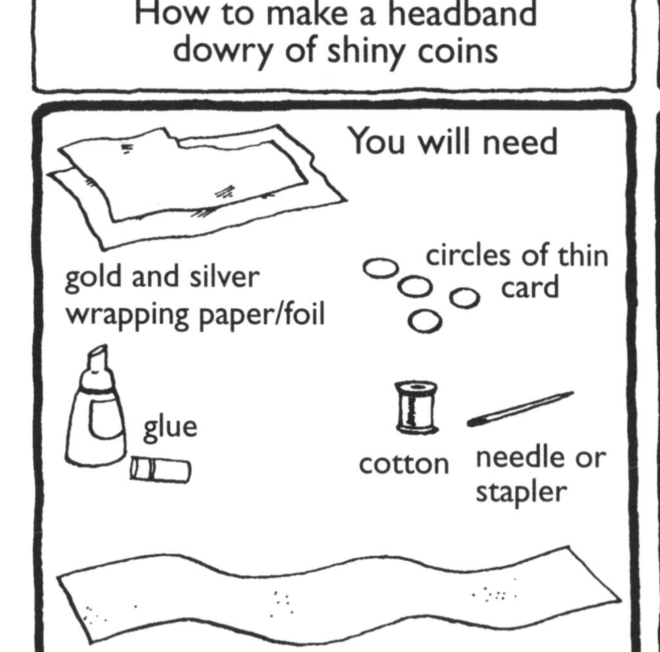

You will need

gold and silver wrapping paper/foil

circles of thin card

glue

cotton

needle or stapler

a band of material (from an old sheet, perhaps) to fit round your head.

What you do

1 Cut round the card circles on the paper and stick the paper to the card.
2 Sew the band of material into a circle that fits your head.
3 Sew the coins on to the front of the band, or staple them
4 Put on the band and wear a head-scarf as shown.

How to make a lost-and-found sheep

You will need

a piece of card tube

this shape of white paper to fit the tube

flap

glue

sheep's wool or cotton wool

2 pipe cleaners

What you do

Draw the face on and stick the flap inside the tube.

Make 4 holes in the bottom of the tube and thread the pipe cleaners through.

Stick wool on the tube and the top of the face.

You can hide your sheep and get your friend to find it.

Luke 15 verse 10

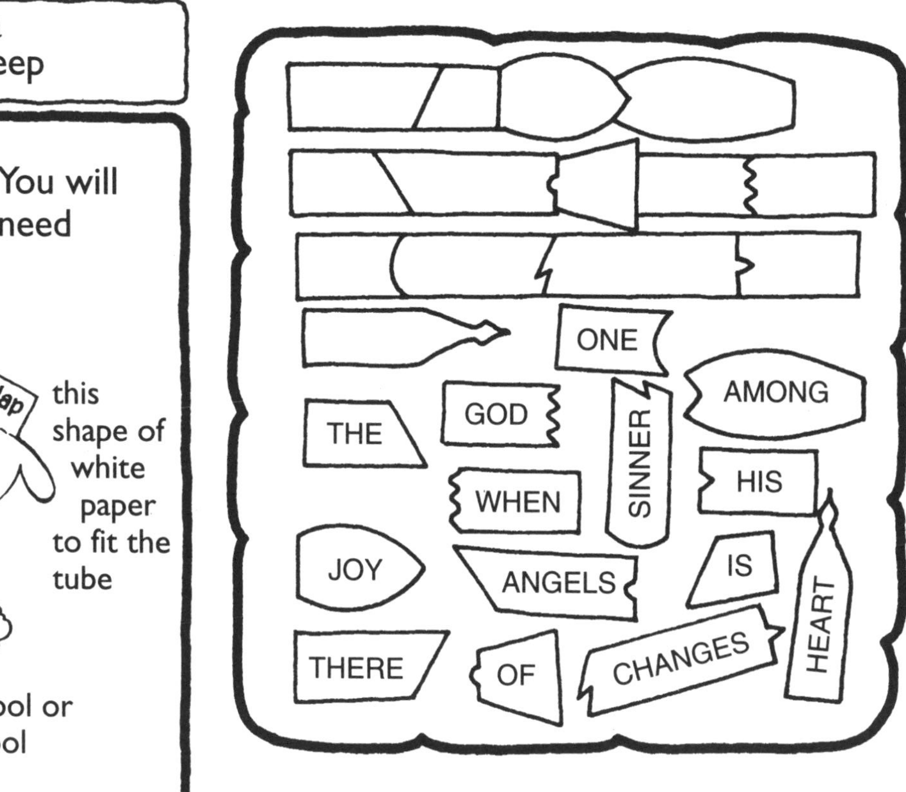

To pray this week

We pray for those who have made wrong choices and cut themselves off from God.
We pray for all those who are living evil lives. May all the lost be found again.
Amen.

Proper 20

Sunday between 18 and 24 September inclusive

Thought for the day

If you cannot be trusted with worldly riches, or even small amounts of money, then you will not be trusted with spiritual riches either.

Readings

Jeremiah 8:18-9:1 or Amos 8:4-7
Psalm 79:1-9 or Psalm 113
1 Timothy 2:1-7
Luke 16:1-13

Aim

To get to know the story of the clever manager, and explore its meaning.

Starter

Who's in charge? One person goes outside the room. The others decide on a leader. Everyone stands in a circle and copies the leader's actions, while the person who was outside tries to guess who the leader is.

Teaching

Today we are going to hear a story Jesus told about someone who was put in charge, and got into a spot of bother.

If possible, use a few costume items, such as a suit jacket for the manager, Hawaiian shirt and shades for the rich man, a large accounts book, a plastic bottle of olive oil, and a bag of flour. First the rich man interviews the manager and gives him the job. They shake hands and the rich man leaves the manager to sort out the accounts. The manager thinks aloud, casually helping himself to the petty cash, and writing it in as expenses. He makes a careful job of forging the rich man's signature on large cheques, pleased that his cheating is going so well, and priding himself on all his skill and hard work at making money like this.

Then the rich man comes in, waving a cheque and saying his bank manager has just shown it to him. He demands a full report and fires the manager. On his own again, the manager makes his plans to ensure he'll be well looked after once he is without a job. He can go to different children and ask them what they owe, looking in his book and saying, 'Now let's see – you owe 3,000 litres of olive oil/ 36,000 litres of flour, I believe?'

The rich man can be creeping behind him, watching what he is doing, and amazed at his cheek. As the manager turns round after the last transaction, he bumps into the rich man, and starts pretending he's been checking up on this person's old mother (or some other con story). The rich man stops him and says he's seen everything. He shakes his hand and laughs, saying something like, 'Well, you're a terrible rogue, and I wouldn't trust you as far as I can jump, but you certainly work hard at it!'

When Jesus told this story, he said that we all know crooks work really hard cadging money from people to get rich; it's a pity that we don't work as hard at getting rich with God's treasures! If we put as much energy into our caring love as that crooked manager put into his cheating, the world would be a much more loving place.

Praying

Dear God,
help us to work hard
at good things
like loving and sharing,
and not to work hard
at bad things
like lying and cheating. Amen.

Activities

On the worksheet there is a blotted page of the accounts book for them to put right, and a checklist of the things in life they work hardest at. They are encouraged to look at the way they spend their pocket money, and to think about giving some away each week to help someone else. Organisations like Christian Aid, Oxfam and Action Aid have children's packs with suggestions for co-operative giving which you could consider.

Notes

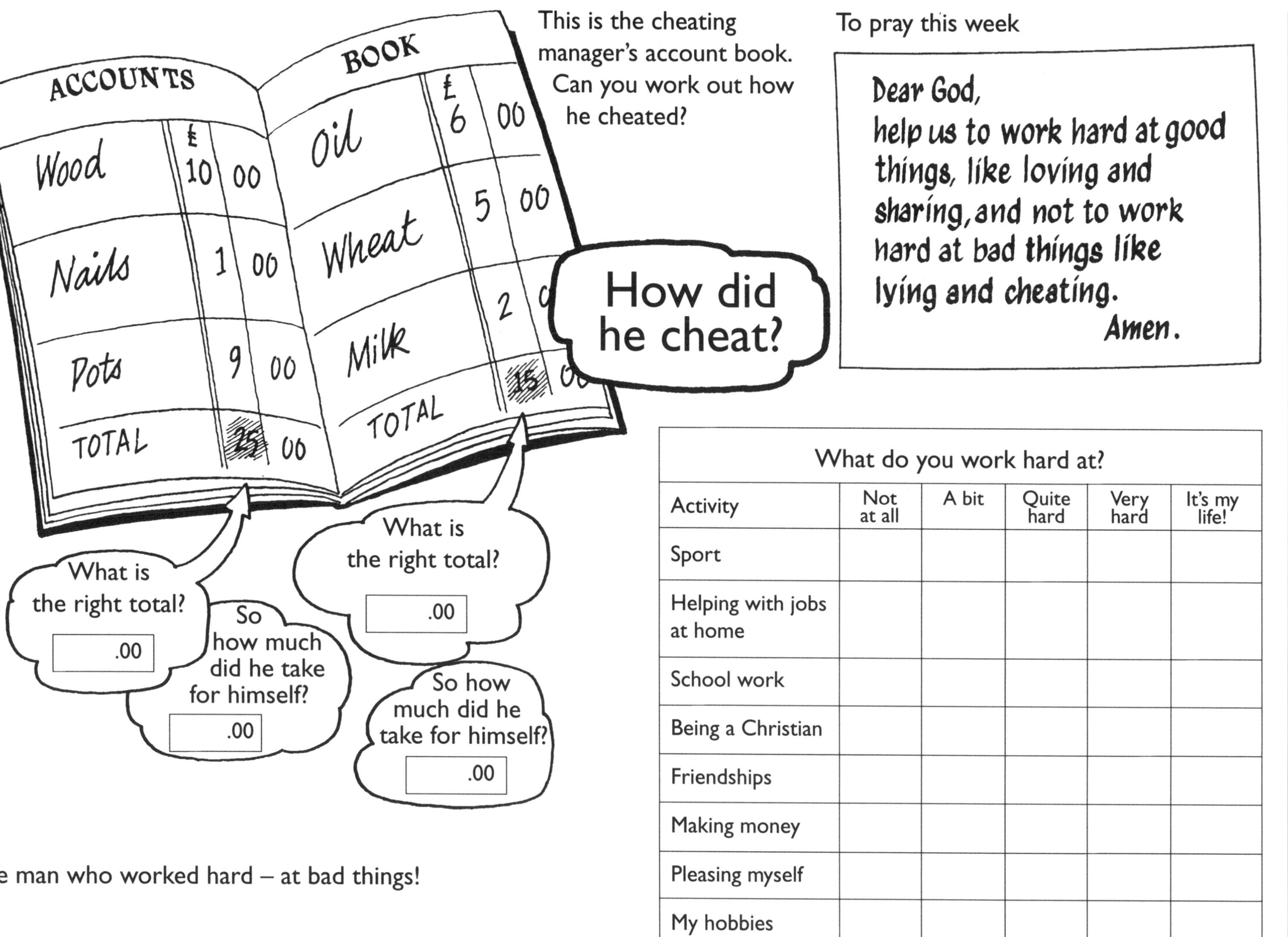

This is the cheating manager's account book. Can you work out how he cheated?

The man who worked hard – at bad things!

To pray this week

Dear God,
help us to work hard at good things, like loving and sharing, and not to work hard at bad things like lying and cheating.
Amen.

What do you work hard at?

Activity	Not at all	A bit	Quite hard	Very hard	It's my life!
Sport					
Helping with jobs at home					
School work					
Being a Christian					
Friendships					
Making money					
Pleasing myself					
My hobbies					

PROPER 21

Sunday between 25 September and 1 October inclusive

Thought for the day

Wealth can make us complacent so that we fail to notice the needs of those around us.

Readings

Jeremiah 32:1-3a, 6-15 or Amos 6:1a, 4-7
Psalm 91:1-6, 14-16 or Psalm 146
1 Timothy 6:6-19
Luke 16:19-31

Aim

To get to know the story of the rich man and Lazarus.

Starter

During a song, arrange for one of the leaders to come in wearing a hat and carrying a trowel, walk across the room and go out again. Don't draw attention to this; ignore it. After the song, ask the children if they noticed anyone coming in during the song, and what they looked like. The person comes in again, and explains that today we are going to hear about someone who didn't take any notice of the needs of someone he saw every day.

Teaching

Use the children to be Lazarus and the rich man, the dogs, the angels and Abraham, as you narrate the story, either directly from the Bible (the New Century *International Children's Bible* is excellent) or in your own words. If you have a spare leader you can go for voice-overs as well.

After the story, talk about what the rich man had done wrong, and how his wealth had made him so comfortable that he didn't notice the needs of others staring him in the face. The children may have some ideas of how the rich man could have done it better.

Praying

Lord, we pray for the poor
and those who don't have enough to eat.
We give you ourselves
for you to use
in helping them. Amen.

Activities

On the sheet they can confirm their commitment to put their faith into practice by drawing someone they can help, and how they plan to do it.

Notes

L	A	Z	A	R	U	S	C	H	U
S	B	A	R	I	T	G	O	O	B
X	R	I	C	C	N	O	M	S	E
G	A	Q	A	H	K	D	F	I	G
B	H	F	B	N	M	E	O	G	G
J	A	T	D	M	G	F	R	U	I
R	M	C	G	A	T	E	T	M	N
Z	L	A	V	N	J	W	L	P	G
Q	K	O	D	H	L	E	Y	S	N
S	U	F	F	E	R	I	N	G	P

Luke 16:19-31

LAZARUS
RICH MAN
GATE
BEGGING
DOGS
ANGELS
ABRAHAM
COMFORT
SUFFERING

Use the words to remind you of the story

To pray this week

Lord, we pray for the poor and those who don't have enough to eat.
We give you ourselves for you to use in helping them.
Amen.

I want to help ______________________________

____

This is how I will help them

PROPER 22

Sunday between 2 and 8 October inclusive

Thought for the day

God hears our distress and our crying, and feels it with us.

Readings

Lamentations 1:1-6 or Habakkuk 1:1-4; 2:1-4
Lamentations 3:19-26 or Psalm 137, or Psalm 37:1-9
2 Timothy 1:1-14
Luke 17:5-10

Aim

To get to know the parable of the servant doing his duty.

Starter

Put on some music, and do a challenging fitness workout, including, perhaps, running on the spot, stepping, skipping, bunny jumps, stretching, and touching toes. Praise them for the way they kept going and kept trying, even when it was hard or tiring.

Teaching

Like our fitness training session, life can sometimes be hard work – such as when we feel jealous of a brother or sister, or when we are finding it difficult to do the work at school, or when there are arguments and rows at home. Collect their ideas and experiences.

How does our God help us at these times, and what tips has Jesus got for coping?

Use simple puppets to act out the story that Jesus told about the servant, doing it the first time with the servant coming in and putting his feet up, and the master protesting that he can't behave like that because he's a servant, not the master. Then make a 'take two' sign and act the situation out with the servant being praised at the end for doing all the jobs. The servant can then protest that he was only doing his duty.

What does the story mean? Jesus says that we are not to expect life to be easy and perfect all the time because it isn't. We can expect there to be sad and difficult times as well as all the happy and easy times. And when they happen, we are to just carry on doing what we know is right, without grumbling too much. God will be there with us in all the difficult times, so we won't be left alone, and he will give us the strength we need to carry on.

Praying

Set out a train layout, with a tunnel (which can be a shoe box with holes at the ends), a gradient and some points. Start the train round the track as you pray:

When life seems an uphill struggle, Lord,
All: keep me on track with you, Jesus.
When we go through dark and lonely times,
All: keep me on track with you, Jesus.
When we have to make choices about how to behave,
All: keep me on track with you, Jesus. Amen.

Activities

There are instructions on the worksheet for making a spinner to remind them of the need to persevere when times are hard, and there is a Bible study activity for which they will need Bibles.

Notes

To pray this week

When life seems an uphill struggle, Lord, keep me on track with you, Jesus. When we go through dark and lonely times, keep me on track with you, Jesus. When we have to make choices about how to behave, keep me on track with you, Jesus.

Amen.

A	C	D	E	F	G	I	L	N	O	P	R	S	T	U	V	W

2 Timothy 1:1-7

This letter was written by .... to .... , who had a mother called .... and a grandmother called .... Paul always remembered them in his .... Timothy shares his mother's and grandmother's .... Paul wants Timothy to let God's gift .... , as a small flame turns into a ....

HOW TO MAKE A SPINNER

1 Colour the spinner and cut it out.

2 Stick it on to thin card.

3 Poke a cocktail stick through the middle.

KEEP ON PRAYING · KEEP ON TRUSTING · KEEP ON LOVING ·

As your spinner spins, it can remind you to go on and on praying, trusting and loving

PROPER 23

Sunday between 9 and 15 October inclusive

Thought for the day

God can always use even seemingly hopeless situations for good.

Readings

Jeremiah 29:1, 4-7 or 2 Kings 5:1-3, 7-15
Psalm 66:1-12 or Psalm 111
2 Timothy 2:8-15
Luke 17:11-19

Aim

To look at the healing of the lepers and the significance of the one who said 'thank you'.

Starter

Musical chairs, or a similar game, where there is always an odd one out when the music stops. Today we are going to think about ten odd ones out, and one odd one out.

Teaching

Two mothers, dressed up in head cloths, are in a village with their pots, collecting water from the village well. They pass the time of day, and then catch sight of the ten lepers in the distance, wondering who they are shouting to. One of the lepers, Jonas, is the son of one of the women and they talk about how sad they are that he can't live at home any more, and how badly he is missed, and how they have never stopped praying for him to be healed. They see that Jesus, the healer and teacher, is coming towards their village, and has stopped to listen to the lepers.

They wonder if Jesus could possibly be making the lepers better. They watch the lepers running away from Jesus and suddenly realise they are heading for the priest's house and are throwing off their bandages as they run. The women get very excited and soon they see some of the lepers running into their own houses in the village. They must be healed! The women start praising God, and are looking forward to Jonas coming back when they see him running all on his own back up the road to Jesus. What on earth is he doing? Then they see Jonas kneel down in front of Jesus. He is pouring out his thanks to Jesus, who is smiling and sharing Jonas's delight. The two women pick up their pots of water and go off to join them.

Praying

Put up all ten fingers and lower the fingers one by one as you say the first ten words. As you say 'Thank you!' you make a thumbs-up sign with one thumb, representing the thankful leper.

You always make us feel better.
Help us to say, 'Thank you!'

Activities

The worksheet gives instructions for making a pop-up thank-you card. There is also a puzzle for which they will need access to a Bible. This reinforces the week's teaching.

Notes

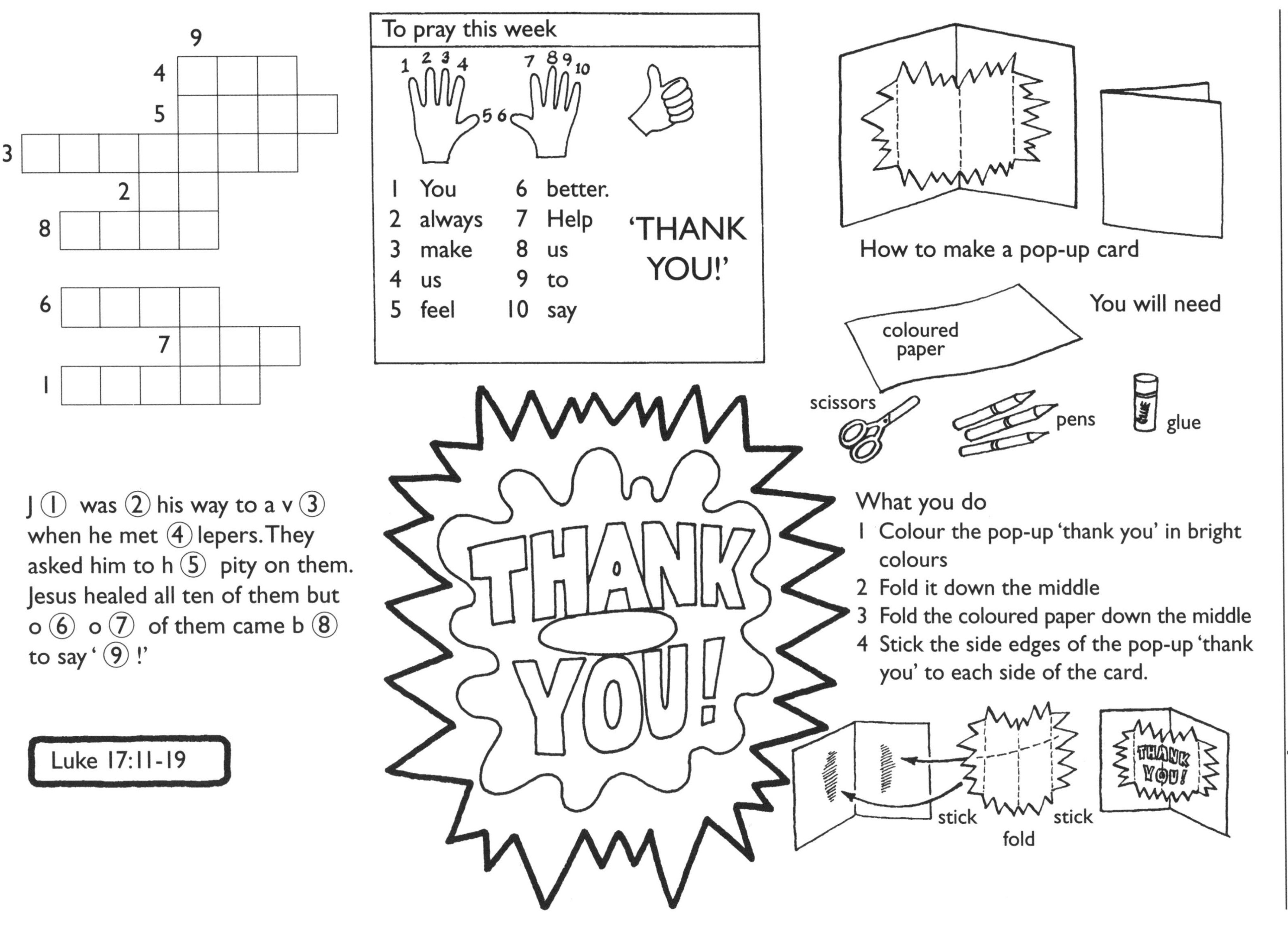
9
4
5
3
2
8
6
7
1
To pray this week
1 2 3 4
5 6
7 8 9 10
1 You
2 always
3 make
4 us
5 feel
6 better.
7 Help
8 us
9 to
10 say
'THANK YOU!'
How to make a pop-up card
You will need
coloured paper
scissors
pens
glue
J ① was ② his way to a v ③ when he met ④ lepers. They asked him to h ⑤ pity on them. Jesus healed all ten of them but o ⑥ o ⑦ of them came b ⑧ to say '⑨!'
Luke 17:11-19
THANK YOU!
What you do
1 Colour the pop-up 'thank you' in bright colours
2 Fold it down the middle
3 Fold the coloured paper down the middle
4 Stick the side edges of the pop-up 'thank you' to each side of the card.
stick
fold
stick
THANK YOU!

Proper 24

Sunday between 16 and 22 October inclusive

Thought for the day

Don't get side-tracked; always pray and don't give up.

Readings

Jeremiah 31:27-34 or Genesis 32:22-31
Psalm 119:97-104 or Psalm 121
2 Timothy 3:14-4:5
Luke 18:1-8

Aim

To learn about perseverance in prayer and Bible-reading.

Starter

Sit in a circle. You start by saying, 'Every morning I say my prayers.' Everyone in turn adds something else to the list of what they do each morning, and repeats all the things that have been already mentioned. This ensures that everyone voices the prayer activity. Also, the separate letters for 'Prayer' and 'Bible-reading' (different colours for each) are hidden around the room, and the children sent to hunt them out. They persevere until they have all the letters and can sort them out into the words.

Teaching

Use the sketch below to introduce the parable of the woman pestering the judge for her rights, and then talk about why they think Jesus told this story.

Woman Knock, knock.

Judge Who's there?

Woman Winnie.

Judge Winnie who?

Woman Winnie you going to do something about that money I was cheated of?

Judge Oh don't worry, that case will be coming up very soon. Now if you don't mind, it's my day off and I'm going to play golf.

(Sign held up saying 'Next day')

Woman Knock, knock.

Judge Who's there?

Woman Winnie.

Judge Winnie who?

Woman Winnie you going to do something about . . .

Judge OK, you don't have to say all that again. I remember. I'll deal with it, madam. Leave it to me. *(Aside)* But not yet because I'd rather watch telly and have a snooze.

Woman Knock, knock.

Judge *(Sounding sleepy)* Who's there?

Woman Winnie.

Judge Winnie who? *(Aside)* Oh, hang on, I won't ask! I don't know, there's no rest for the wicked. Wretched woman, I'd better do what she asks or I'll never get any peace! *(Shouts)* All right, Winnie, you win. I'll come with you and sort it out *now*!

What is the story saying to us? Point out that Jesus was saying, 'If even a lazy old judge like that eventually listened to the woman, we can be certain that our loving God will listen to us straight away every time, and answer our prayer.' Sometimes his answer might be that we have to wait, or that what we are asking for wouldn't help us forward as much as we think it would.

Have an alarm clock, a knife and fork and spoon, a musical box lullaby, and a toothbrush and toothpaste.

Set them down and talk about these as being the times to remember to pray, so that we are sure to be praying at least at these times. It doesn't have to take hours, but we do need to make contact with God several times each day. Put a praying logo next to all of the items, and an open Bible in front of them, asking them to think of the best time for them to do this.

Show them some suitable daily Bible-reading aids and invite parents to look at some Bible translations you recommend. (See page 9 for those I have found useful.)

Praying

Use the symbols from the teaching.

Lord God, I want to keep in touch with you
all through the day.

Help me to remember that in the morning

ring the alarm

before I eat

clash the knife and fork

and before I go to sleep

play the lullaby or brush teeth

I can talk to you and know you are listening.

Activities

The worksheet helps them make a week's chart to set them off on the praying and Bible-reading habit, for which they can be rewarded next week.

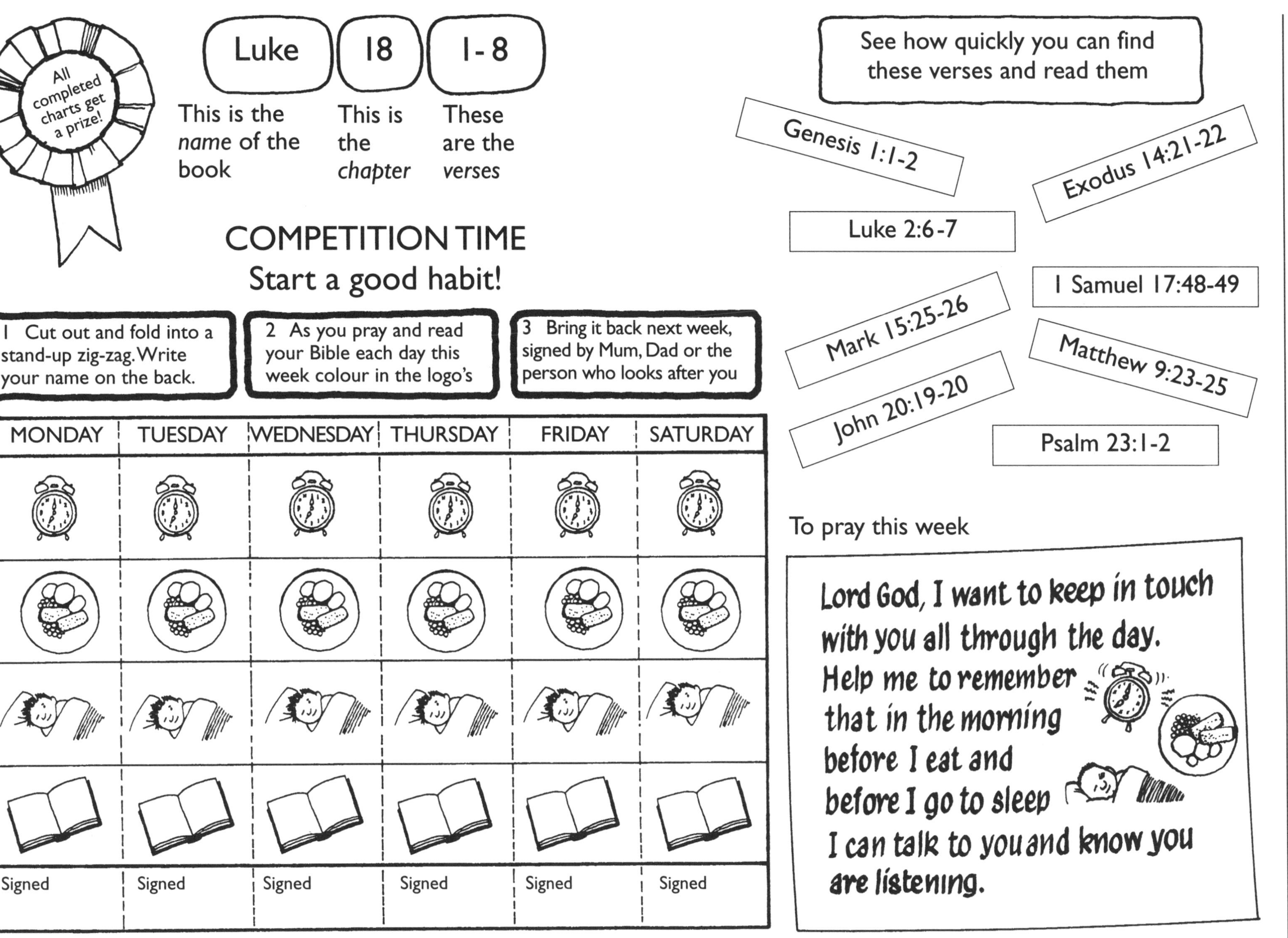
All completed charts get a prize!
Luke
18
1-8
This is the *name* of the book
This is the *chapter*
These are the *verses*
COMPETITION TIME
Start a good habit!
1 Cut out and fold into a stand-up zig-zag. Write your name on the back.
2 As you pray and read your Bible each day this week colour in the logo's
3 Bring it back next week, signed by Mum, Dad or the person who looks after you
MONDAY
TUESDAY
WEDNESDAY
THURSDAY
FRIDAY
SATURDAY
Signed
Signed
Signed
Signed
Signed
Signed
See how quickly you can find these verses and read them
Genesis 1:1-2
Exodus 14:21-22
Luke 2:6-7
1 Samuel 17:48-49
Mark 15:25-26
Matthew 9:23-25
John 20:19-20
Psalm 23:1-2
To pray this week
Lord God, I want to keep in touch
with you all through the day.
Help me to remember
that in the morning
before I eat and
before I go to sleep
I can talk to you and know you
are listening.

PROPER 25

Sunday between 23 and 29 October inclusive

Thought for the day

When we recognise our dependence on God we will approach him with true humility and accept his gifts with joy.

Readings

Joel 2:23-32 or Ecclesiasticus 35:12-17 or
Jeremiah 14:7-10, 19-22
Psalm 65 or Psalm 84:1-7
2 Timothy 4:6-8, 16-18
Luke 18:9-14

Aim

To get to know the parable from Luke 18:9-14 and learn about being right with God.

Starter

A 'getting it right' game, such as sticking the tail on the donkey, blindfold, or using some conkers to roll on to a board with numbered squares on it. Where your conker lands is your score.

Teaching

Explain that Jesus found some people he was with were always looking down on others, and making out they were much better than everyone else. They seemed to have forgotten that they owed their whole life to God. Jesus didn't like to see that, and it made him sad. So he told them this story to show them how they were behaving, hoping it would make them realise what they were doing and try to change.

Use simple puppets, made out of wooden spoons or spatulas, to tell the story. The pictures below will help you with the expressions. Then talk about which one of the two went home right with God, and why. Reinforce that we all depend on God for our life, and everything comes from him. Read Psalm 65:9-13 and enjoy celebrating our love for our wonderful God.

Praying

You know us, Lord,
so we can't pretend with you.
You shower us with blessings
like a shower of rain;
you give us your power
to make us grow more loving
all through our lives.

Activities

On the worksheet there are instructions for making a rain mobile. The children will need cotton wool, card, cotton, shiny blue and silver wrapping paper, and a tiny bell each. If you want the raindrops to be stronger, they can be thickened with card raindrop shapes.

Notes

How to make a rain mobile

You will need

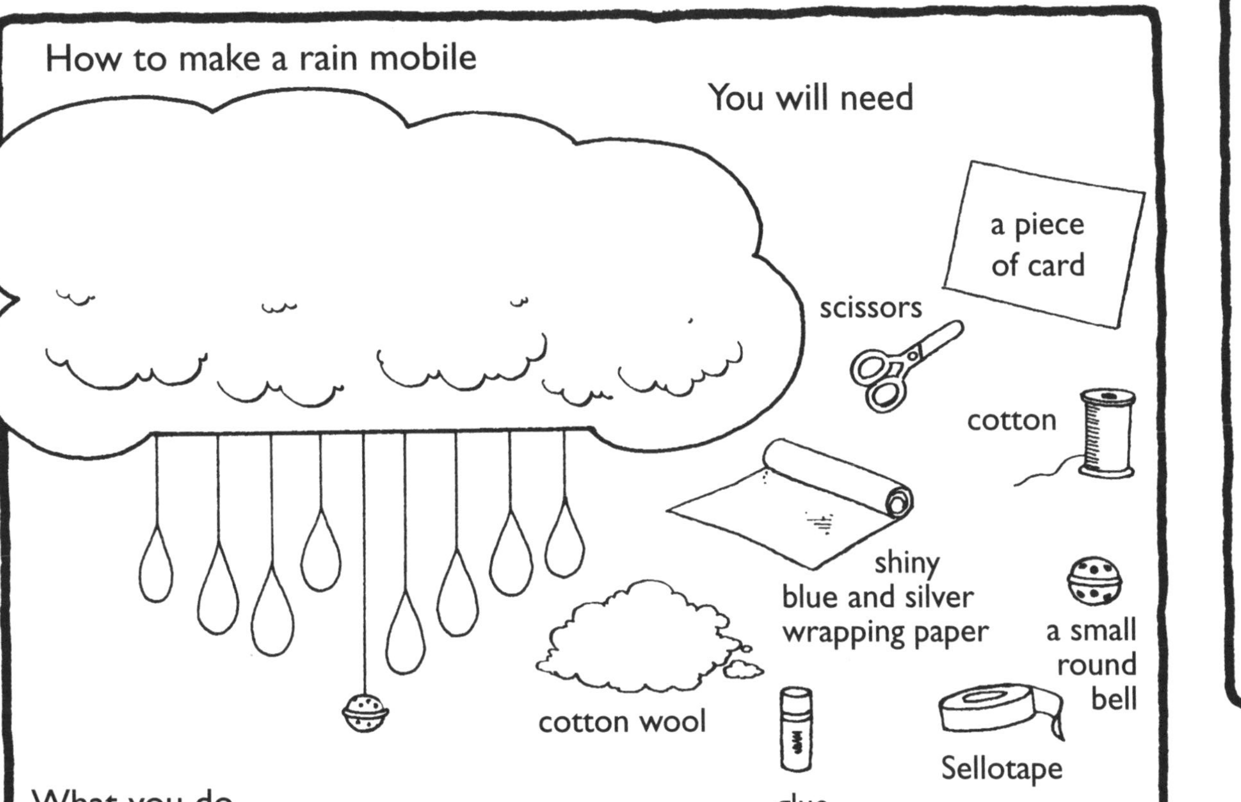

What you do

1 Cut the card into the shape of a cloud.
2 Stick cotton wool on one side.
3 Fold the shiny blue and silver wrapping paper in half, and cut out pairs of raindrops.
4 Place a piece of cotton in the middle of each pair and sandwich them together with glue.
5 Stick the other ends of the cotton to the back of the cloud with Sellotape.
6 Tie a piece of cotton to the bell and Sellotape the other end to the cloud.
7 Sellotape another piece of cotton to the top of the cloud, and hang your mobile up. It will remind you of the love God showers us with.

You take care of the land and water it.
Psalm 65:9

On 1 ear of corn there are ______ grains.

On 5 ears of corn there are ______ grains.

On 10 ears of corn there are ______ grains.

On 100 ears of corn there are ______ grains.

To pray this week

You know us, Lord, so we
can't pretend with you.
You shower us with blessings
like a shower of rain;
You give us your power to
make us grow more loving
all through our lives.

All Saints' Day

Sunday between 30 October and 5 November inclusive

Thought for the day

In Christ we are chosen to be God's holy people.

Readings

Daniel 7:1-3, 15-18
Psalm 149
Ephesians 1:11-23
Luke 6:20-31

Aim

To learn about what it means to be a saint.

Starter

Have a quiz by sticking pictures of well-known saints around the walls. Give the children a list of the saints' names and a few facts about them. They have to try and match up the picture with the saint. Here are some possible ones to choose: your parish saint, Peter, Francis, Catherine, George, Nicholas and Mary.

Teaching

Talk about all these saints being friends of God. You aren't born a saint, and you don't suddenly wake up one morning to find you have turned into a saint. Becoming a saint happens naturally as you open yourself more and more to God's love, and let him into your life. People become saints by living their lives closely with God so that his Holy Spirit fills them.

We often hear about saints when lots of people have met them and heard about the way they lived. Their stories have helped many people to know and love God more. Sometimes their stories of bravery have helped other people to be brave; or their stories of kindness and honesty have helped other people to be kind and honest.

God has promised that all his friends will live with him in the joy and loveliness of heaven when they die. Whenever we praise and worship God on earth, we are joined by all those praising and worshipping him in heaven.

Praying

Lord, make me an instrument of your peace.
Where there is hatred, let me sow love;
where there is injury, pardon;
where there is doubt, faith;
where there is darkness, light;
where there is despair, hope,
and where there is sadness, joy.
(From a prayer of Saint Francis)

Activities

Using the worksheet pattern and illustrations, make a book of saints which opens out into the shape of a cross.

Notes

Colour
the pictures, then fold up
like this:
Tuck 5 round
the back of 0
and draw on
the title:
SAINTS ARE FILLED
WITH GOD'S LOVE.
2
1
0
4
5
3
Lord, make me an instrument of your peace.
Where there is hatred, let me sow love;
where there is injury, pardon; where there is
doubt, faith; where there is darkness, light;
where there is despair, hope, and where
there is sadness, joy.
Cut along thick lines
Fold along dotted lines
Whenever you look
at your saints book you
see the cross – the sign
of God's love
This week's prayer was
prayed by Saint Francis

FOURTH SUNDAY BEFORE ADVENT

*Sunday between 30 October and 5 November inclusive**

* For use if the Feast of All Saints was celebrated on 1 November and alternative propers are needed.

Thought for the day

Jesus came to search out the lost and save them. Through him we come to our senses and make our lives clean.

Readings

Isaiah 1:10-18
Psalm 32:1-7
2 Thessalonians 1:1-12
Luke 19:1-10

Aim

To learn about the fun of being forgiven and having a fresh start.

Starter

Bring a selection of chalkboards, chalk and dampened cloths, magic slates (which let you erase what you have written), white board, pens and cleaning cloth, and sand trays. Have a time of free play with these, so they can enjoy the satisfaction of drawing and erasing and starting again.

Teaching

Talk about what they have been doing, and the fun of being able to start again whenever you make a mistake. Sometimes we make mistakes and do things that are wrong, and we wish they could be rubbed out as well as our drawings today.

Well, with Jesus, they can! Today we are going to hear about someone who met Jesus and was able to make a completely fresh start.

Tell the story of Zacchaeus using cut-out pictures on a background of carpet tiles or towels. The children can help place the houses and trees, and the crowd of people. As you tell the story, get the children to imagine what the other people were thinking when Jesus noticed the cheating tax collector, what Zacchaeus was thinking when he was noticed, and how he felt when he made a fresh start.

Praying

Lord my God,
you and I both know
the mistakes I make in life.
Please rub them out for me,
and forgive me all my sins
so that I can make a fresh start,
starting today.

Activities

On the worksheet there are instructions for making a tree with Zacchaeus in it (using a flap), and a cartoon story to remind them of how good it feels to be forgiven and start afresh.

Notes

Tim has rubbed out his mistakes.
Can you draw in the bits he got wrong?
Zacchaeus! Hu up and come dc
1. Oliver wanted to be in the gang. "You can't be in it unless you steal some sweets" they said.
2. After school Oliver went to the sweet shop. He managed to steal a Mars bar without the shopkeeper seeing.
3. They let him join the gang. Oliver was proud to be in. But he kept feeling bad about the stealing.
4. He worried about it in bed and at school. He knew it was wrong and he kept pretending it was OK to steal.
5. At last he told his Dad. It felt so good to have got rid of the worry. Dad went with him to the shop and he paid for the Mars bar. He felt HAPPY!!
Colour the tree and the flap. Fold the flap and push through the slit
To pray together
Lord my God, you and I both know the mistakes I make in life. Please rub them out for me, and forgive me all my sins so that I can make a fresh start, starting today!

THIRD SUNDAY BEFORE ADVENT

Sunday between 6 and 12 November inclusive

Thought for the day

Life after death is not wishful thinking but a definite reality.

Readings

Job 19:23-27a
Psalm 17:1-9
2 Thessalonians 2:1-5, 13-17
Luke 20:27-38

Aim

To stretch our minds to imagine things beyond our physical sight.

Starter

Put on some praise music on tape, and do lots of strenuous stretching exercises to the music, till their bodies are well and truly stretched.

Teaching

Explain that we have been stretching our bodies and now we are going to stretch our minds as well. (Don't rush this journey – shut your own eyes and actually imagine it as you direct them and that will get the timing right.) Get them to shut their eyes and imagine their town all around them . . . and beyond that all the countryside stretching out to the sea all around them . . . imagine the round world curving away from where they are sitting so they are riding on the ball-shaped planet earth through space, going slowly round the brilliant sun. Take them on a speeded up reverse journey to end up back in (St Andrew's) hall, where they can open their eyes.

Even though we don't usually think about it or imagine it, we are actually doing that journey all the time! We really are perched on the outside of a planet, riding through space around the sun.

Jesus liked to get people to stretch their minds. There is so much that we can't see because it's too huge, or too minute, or simply invisible. We can't see heaven but Jesus told his friends that there definitely is life after death, and when we die we will know exactly what it is like.

For the moment, though, while we live bound by things like time and space, we can only imagine how wonderful and brilliant heaven will be.

Some people, both now and then, didn't believe in life after death. They came to Jesus and asked him a tricky question. (You can either use children or lego-type people for this)

There was this woman (choose a girl to stand up) and she got married (choose a boy to stand). Then the husband died (boy falls down) so she married someone else (another boy stands up) . . . Carry on for seven husbands. Now at the resurrection (all the dead husbands stand up again), who is the woman going to be married to? (The girl pretends to look very puzzled.)

Let everyone sit down again. The people asking the question thought Jesus would have to agree that life after death was a silly idea. But he didn't. Jesus told them that they were expecting life in heaven to carry on in just the same way as life on earth, but it's not like that. In heaven there won't be things like who's married to whom, because we will be like angels, just happy to be God's children.

Praying

And our eyes at last shall see him
through his own redeeming love.
For that child, so dear and gentle,
is our Lord in heaven above.
And he leads his children on
to the place where he is gone.

Activities

On the sheet there are some examples of the 'tasters' of heaven we are given on earth, and space for them to include others. There are also some mind-stretching puzzles.

Notes

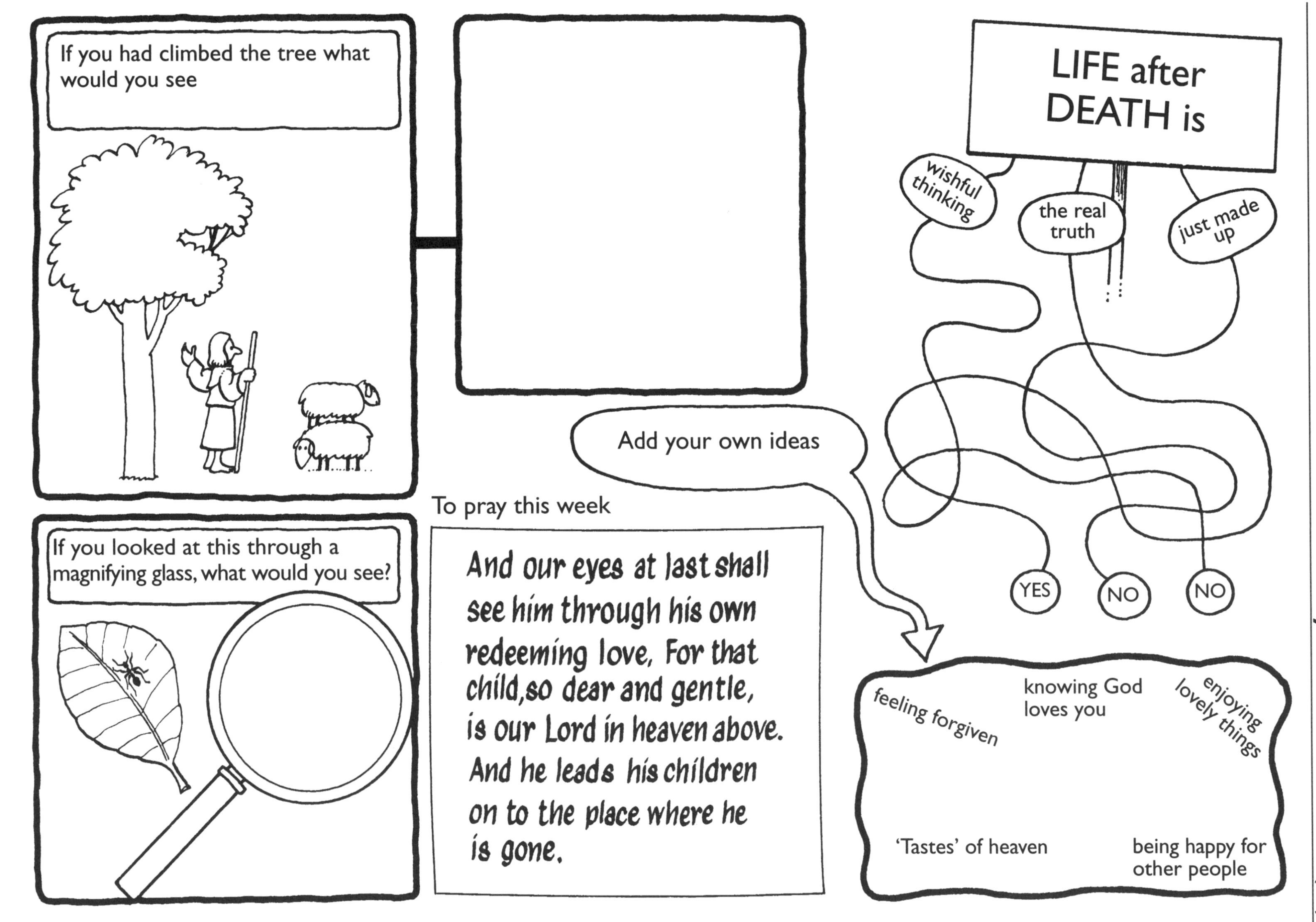
If you had climbed the tree what would you see
If you looked at this through a magnifying glass, what would you see?
Add your own ideas
To pray this week
And our eyes at last shall see him through his own redeeming love, For that child, so dear and gentle, is our Lord in heaven above. And he leads his children on to the place where he is gone.
LIFE after DEATH is
wishful thinking
the real truth
just made up
YES
NO
NO
feeling forgiven
knowing God loves you
enjoying lovely things
'Tastes' of heaven
being happy for other people

SECOND SUNDAY BEFORE ADVENT

Sunday between 13 and 19 November inclusive

Thought for the day

There will be dark and dangerous times as the end approaches, but by standing firm through it all we will gain life.

Readings

Malachi 4:1-2a
Psalm 98
2 Thessalonians 3:6-13
Luke 21:5-19

Aim

To know that standing firm to the end is hard but worthwhile.

Starter

No yes, no no. Try to answer everyone's questions without using the words 'yes' and 'no'.

Teaching

Look at some examples of signs that tell us about things that are going to happen, like posters to advertise plays and concerts, road signs, weather signs (such as 'red sky at night, shepherds' delight', and cloud formations) and illness signs (such as feeling hot and shaky, or having a rash).

Today we are going to hear about the signs which Jesus said would mark the coming of the last age before all things are completed at the end of time.

Have ready a large sheet titled: 'Signs of the last age', and pictures to represent the signs and events, which are fixed on to the sheet as they are mentioned. You can use the pictures below.

Point out that we are in the last age at the moment, as we live between the Resurrection and the Second Coming.

Jesus warned his friends that this would be a difficult and dangerous age to live in and stay faithful to God. And that is true. Since Jesus said these words, lots of his followers have been arrested and imprisoned.

At this point, have a leader bursting into the room with some plastic handcuffs, without smiling, and very officious. Is there a (Thomas Godsill) here? They have reason to believe that this man is a Christian and they've come to arrest him. The other leaders protest, in a frightened way, that there aren't any Christians here, but Thomas (forewarned and primed, of course) stands out and proclaims that yes, he is a Christian, and worships the living God! The police angrily grab and arrest him, putting him in prison, behind a row of chairs.

Hopefully this episode will take the children by surprise so that they get a sense of danger, but without being unduly scared.

Jesus promised that though being his followers may involve getting teased or even imprisoned and tortured, we will always have Jesus' companionship, and 'by standing firm, you will gain life'.

Praying

O Jesus, I have promised
to serve thee to the end;
be thou for ever near me,
my Master and my friend;
I shall not fear the battle
if thou art by my side,
nor wander from the pathway
if thou wilt be my guide.

Activities

Make a group banner or poster to express the darkness and dangers, with candle flames of light to represent people living out good Christian lives in the middle of it. These form a winding path through the turmoil to a burst of light at the top of the picture.

THXEYXXWXILXLXDXOXXALXLXTHXESXEXTHXIXNGXSXTXOXXYOXUXBECXAXUSEXYOXUXFXOLXLOXWXMXEX
Cross out the crosses to read Luke 21:12
To pray this week
O Jesus, I have promised
to serve thee to the end;
be thou for ever near me,
my Master and my friend;
I shall not fear the battle
if thou art by my side, nor
wander from the pathway
if thou wilt be my guide.
Luke 21:18-19
TQP HJHF JI PMFOF PMBHRO
ASH NFSEEX MSNG XJQ. TX
OPSHYBHR IBNG XJQ VBEE
RSBH EBIF.
A B C D E F G H I J K L M N O P Q R S T U V W X Y Z
S T A Y F I R M B C D E G H J K L N O P Q U V W X Z
CODE
Crack the Code

Christ the King

Sunday between 20 and 26 November inclusive

Thought for the day

This Jesus, dying by crucifixion between criminals, is the anointed King of all creation in whom all things are reconciled.

Readings

Jeremiah 23:1-6
Psalm 46
Colossians 1:11-20
Luke 23:33-43

Aim

To explore the kind of King Jesus is.

Starter

What/who am I? Someone thinks of a person or thing, and the others ask questions to discover who or what it is. Only yes and no answers are allowed.

Teaching

In that game we were finding out more and more about the person or object until we were sure we knew who or what it was. Write up the name 'Jesus' in large letters in the middle of a sheet of paper and write around it all the things we have discovered about Jesus in our lives so far. Already we know quite a bit about him, and we are getting to know him in person as well. Encourage them to keep on their praying every day, and see if any of them have still got a prayer habit, and are using their prayer corner that they made this year. If we've got a bit slack, let's get that going again.

Today we are celebrating Jesus Christ as King. What kind of a King is Jesus?

On another sheet, with a crown with Jesus' name on it in the middle, collect their ideas about this, prompting them if necessary with suggestions of things Jesus isn't, like bossy, proud, or greedy. Then draw a cross going through the crown; the cross is a better sign for our King because all the things we've written are to do with love, which he showed by dying for us on the cross.

Read them today's Gospel to remind ourselves of just how loving and forgiving our King is.

Praying

When I survey the wondrous cross
on which the Prince of Glory died,
my richest gain I count but loss,
and pour contempt on all my pride.

Were the whole realm of nature mine
that were an offering far too small;
love so amazing, so divine,
demands my soul, my life, my all.

Activities

On the worksheet there are instructions for making a jigsaw in which the central piece which holds the rest together is in the shape of a cross.

Notes

1. Cut out the rectangle. On the blank side, draw and colour a picture of something which makes you very happy. Fill the whole page.
2. Cut up your picture along the lines shown; you should have 8 pieces.
3. Stick these pieces on thin card to make them strong.
4. As you put your puzzle together, remember that Jesus our king brings us back together with God. When we fall apart he puts us together again.

To pray this week

When I survey the wondrous cross
on which the Prince of Glory died,
my richest gain I count but loss,
and pour contempt on all my pride.
Were the whole realm of nature mine
that were an offering far too small;
love so amazing, so divine,
demands my soul, my life, my all.

Dictionary

Survey – look at

Contempt – scorn, something you don't think much of

Realm – kingdom

Offering – a present

Divine – just like God

Demands – asks

Waiting for your Spirit

Text: Mick Gisbey
Music: Mick Gisbey, arr. Noel Rawsthorne